Homelessness Issues

Editor: Tina Brand

Volume 336

Independence Educational Publishers

First published by Independence Educational Publishers

The Studio, High Green

Great Shelford

Cambridge CB22 5EG

England

© Independence 2018

Copyright

Photocopy licence

ISBN-13: 978 1 86168 787 6

Printed in Great Britain

Zenith Print Group

Contents

Introduction

HOMELESSNESS ISSUES is Volume 336 in the **ISSUES** series. The aim of the series is to offer current, diverse information about important issues in our world, from a UK perspective.

ABOUT HOMELESSNESS

Since the onset of austerity in 2010, the estimated number of people sleeping rough in England has more than doubled, from 1,768 in 2010, to 4,134 in 2016. As the number of homeless people increases, while support services and hostels are diminishing, rough sleepers are becoming ever more visible in British cities. This book explores the many reasons why people become homeless. It also considers the impact homelessness can have on a person's physical and mental health. It also explores the ways in we can reduce the number of homeless people in the UK.

OUR SOURCES

Titles in the **ISSUES** series are designed to function as educational resource books, providing a balanced overview of a specific subject.

The information in our books is comprised of facts, articles and opinions from many different sources, including:

⇨ Newspaper reports and opinion pieces

⇨ Website factsheets

⇨ Magazine and journal articles

⇨ Statistics and surveys

⇨ Government reports

⇨ Literature from special interest groups.

A NOTE ON CRITICAL EVALUATION

Because the information reprinted here is from a number of different sources, readers should bear in mind the origin of the text and whether the source is likely to have a particular bias when presenting information (or when conducting their research). It is hoped that, as you read about the many aspects of the issues explored in this book, you will critically evaluate the information presented.

It is important that you decide whether you are being presented with facts or opinions. Does the writer give a biased or unbiased report? If an opinion is being expressed, do you agree with the writer? Is there potential bias to the 'facts' or statistics behind an article?

ASSIGNMENTS

In the back of this book, you will find a selection of assignments designed to help you engage with the articles you have been reading and to explore your own opinions. Some tasks will take longer than others and there is a mixture of design, writing and research-based activities that you can complete alone or in a group.

FURTHER RESEARCH

At the end of each article we have listed its source and a website that you can visit if you would like to conduct your own research. Please remember to critically evaluate any sources that you consult and consider whether the information you are viewing is accurate and unbiased.

Useful weblinks

www.24housing.co.uk

www.uk.depaulcharity.org

www.theconversation.com

www.theguardian.com

www.gov.uk

www.huffingtonpost.co.uk

www.independent.co.uk

www.jfr.org.uk

www.politics.co.uk

www.shelter.org.uk

www.telegraph.co.uk

www.thirdforcenews.org.uk

What is homelessness?

You may be homeless if you're sleeping rough, don't have rights to stay where you are or you live in unsuitable housing.

When are you homeless?

The definition of homelessness means not having a home. You are homeless if you have nowhere to stay and are living on the streets, but you can be homeless even if you have a roof over your head.

You count as homeless if you are:

⇨ staying with friends or family

⇨ staying in a hostel, night shelter or B&B

⇨ squatting (because you have no legal right to stay)

⇨ at risk of violence or abuse in your home

⇨ living in poor conditions that affect your health

⇨ living apart from your family because you don't have a place to live together.

Who is affected?

Homelessness affects a wide variety of people. Some people may be more vulnerable to homelessness.

You may be more at risk if you are:

⇨ leaving home for the first time or leaving care

⇨ pregnant with nowhere to stay when the baby comes

⇨ struggling to live on benefits or a low income

⇨ from abroad without the right to claim benefits

⇨ an asylum seeker or refugee

⇨ leaving prison.

How do people become homeless?

You could become homeless for many different reasons. These could include:

⇨ being evicted

⇨ splitting up with your partner

⇨ family or friends asking you to leave

⇨ domestic violence or abuse

⇨ harassment by neighbours

⇨ a disaster such as a fire or flooding.

Who can help if you are homeless?

You can ask for help from a local council if you are homeless or threatened with homelessness.

Local councils have a legal duty to help some people. Not everyone gets help with housing, some people just get advice on how to find a home.

Usually it's the housing department that helps, but sometimes social services helps instead. This may happen if the housing department can't help but there are children in the family or someone is elderly or frail.

Some charities for the homeless may help young people, people who don't have children and people with drug or alcohol problems. Some provide temporary emergency accommodation such as night-shelters or hostels.

A local church or charity may also be able to help with basics like food and clothing. Practical help is provided by day centres for homeless people, food banks and soup runs.

Get advice if you are homeless or at risk

Get advice as soon as possible if you are homeless or worried about becoming homeless.

A housing adviser might be able to help you to:

⇨ find a way to stay in your home

⇨ find a new home more quickly

⇨ get help from your local council

You can get advice from Shelter, your local Citizen's Advice or law centre.

1 January 2016

⇨ The above information is reprinted with kind permission from Shelter. Please visit www.shelter.org.uk for further information.

© Shelter 2018

Half a century of homelessness in the UK – here's what has changed

An article from **The Conversation.**

THE CONVERSATION

By Graham Bowpitt, Reader in Social Policy, Nottingham Trent University

Injury, unemployment, eviction, squats, shelters, social services – homelessness. This is the desperate spiral depicted in Ken Loach's influential film, *Cathy Come Home*. First aired 50 years ago, the drama offers a graphic portrayal of the treatment of an ordinary family by public authorities, as they grapple with homelessness.

Reflecting the public outrage at the film's revelations, the pressure group Shelter was founded to raise awareness and campaign for reform. The same year saw the publication of one of the only government-sponsored surveys of homelessness in England, by the National Assistance Board (NAB).

On the 50th anniversary of these three landmark events, it's time to ask whether Cathy and her family would suffer the same tragedies today.

The first count

We're not shown what happens to Cathy after her children are taken by social services. In all likelihood, she would have joined the 965 people sleeping rough, which the NAB found in their one-night head count on 6 December, 1965, of which only 45 were women.

She could have become one of the 1,367 unaccommodated claimants of National Assistance, the precursor to our Jobseekers Allowance. That meagre provision might then have afforded her the occasional bed in one of the 567 commercial or charitable hostels and lodging houses, which housed 28,789 inhabitants, of which just 1,905 were women.

Free, public sector accommodation was limited to the NAB's own reception centres – a relic from the Victorian era's Poor Law workhouses – which housed 1,956 men at the time of the count.

After computing these figures, the survey estimated that there were about 13,500 single homeless people in December 1965, the vast majority of whom would have been men.

Ten years on

Cathy might have fared better a decade later. Tireless campaigning by Shelter and other charities finally bore fruit, in the form of the 1977 Housing (Homeless Persons) Act. The act is unique among Western states, because it makes housing a statutory right for certain people.

The law obliges local authorities to provide permanent housing to families who are judged to be "unintentionally homeless" (or threatened with homelessness) and belong to a "priority need group". These include families with dependent children or pregnant women.

So, Cathy would have had housing rights up to the point where her children were removed by social services, although she would still need to prove that she had not become homeless "intentionally", by being evicted from a private tenancy for failing to keep up rent payments. Despite several re-enactments, these laws have withstood Thatcherism, and today remain in more or less their original form.

Yet any expectations that the act has worked to eliminate homelessness today must be quickly disappointed. The methods used by the NAB to count homelessness have changed over time, which makes comparisons tricky. But figures released by the Department for Communities and Local Government, based on nightly head counts undertaken in the autumn of 2015, revealed 3,569 rough sleepers. This is double the number recorded in 2010, and nearly five times the figure quoted 50 years ago.

Services have not expanded to cope. The NAB counted 34,596 available places in hostel accommodation in 1966. The charity Homeless Link recorded 36,540 in 2014.

Would Cathy still lose her children for being homeless in 2016? An investigation for Inside Housing revealed that 35 of the 106 councils that responded to their survey had taken at least one child into care during 2014/15, where the main reason was homelessness. This tells us that a third of councils are still pursuing

this practice, 50 years after Cathy and nearly 40 years after legislation was supposed to make it unnecessary.

Ray of hope

Amid this darkening outlook, some hope rests with the Homelessness Reduction Bill, which is currently being debated in parliament. As it stands, the bill will oblige local authorities to assist all homeless people by assessing their situation, helping to prevent their homelessness where possible, or providing temporary accommodation for up to 56 days.

It also addresses the most rapidly increasing trigger of homelessness: the shorthold tenancy. When a shorthold tenancy comes to an end – usually after a period of six months – the landlord can evict the tenant without any legal reason. The new bill requires that local authorities treat households as "threatened with homelessness", as soon as an eviction notice is served. This means people like Cathy won't have to wait for the bailiffs to arrive before help is available.

If the NAB enumerators were to repeat their survey today, they would be struck by how little has changed. Some comparisons are possible using data on rough sleepers compiled by the Mayor of London's office. Compared with 50 years ago, today's rough sleeping population is younger, more female and more vulnerable. It has a greater proportion of foreign nationals, and as we have seen, it is larger and growing by the year.

But unaffordable and insecure tenancies remain the primary reason that people are left without accommodation. The proposed legislation offers some hope, but its provisions are essentially reactive – until politicians address the underlying causes, people like Cathy will continue to struggle.

20 December 2016

⇨ The above information is reprinted with kind permission from *The Conversation*. Please visit www. theconversation.com for further information.

© 2010-2018, The Conversation Trust (UK)

Benefit freeze leaves families facing steep rent rise or eviction, Shelter warns

Teachers and other public sector workers risk homelessness.

By Toby Helm

Families who rely on state help to pay their rent will have to find hundreds of pounds extra every month to avoid eviction because of the government's freeze on housing benefit, the homeless charity Shelter has warned.

Demands from Shelter and other housing organisations for a Government rethink come as a number of local authorities – mostly in the south of England – report that many of those being evicted and rendered homeless are now in full-time work, typically in public sector jobs such as teaching or nursing.

Ahead of this week's budget, the charities are calling on ministers to end the freeze, which is set to run until 2020, and to build more affordable homes in areas of need, or to risk a further explosion in the already rapidly rising numbers being placed in costly emergency accommodation by their local authorities.

One single mother of two young children in north London who works full time as a teacher told *The Observer* she had always thought her job, and contribution to the community, would ensure she could find a respectable home. Instead, after her partner left and her landlord put up the rent to a level she could not afford on her own, she was evicted. She is now living at a B&B in east London where her children have no room to play.

"It is really sad that there is nothing available for someone in my position," she said. "I genuinely thought that being a teacher I would be OK. To think that the Government cannot do

better for me and my children is really terrible."

The new research by Shelter has found that in one in four areas of England, the combination of rising rents and the benefit freeze means families with one or two children living in a two-bedroom rented home and claiming housing benefit will have to find at least £100 extra rent a month over the next year.

In many parts of southern England the shortfalls will be more than £200 a month. In London they will rise in areas such as Tower Hamlets, Greenwich and Hackney to nearer £400 a month. In Camden, the shortfall will be over £600 a month, rising to £1,252 in Kensington and Chelsea.

The housing benefit cap was first announced by George Osborne as part of a drive to cut £10 billion from the benefits bill. But the policy is backfiring, and hitting those in work and landing local authorities with the bill for emergency housing for the homeless.

The number of households that have become homeless after an eviction over the past year is up 12% compared with a year ago at 18,820 while the total number of households in temporary accommodation has risen to 74,630, up 9% on a year earlier. Eviction by private landlord is now the most common cause of homelessness.

Roger Harding, director of communications, policy and campaigns at Shelter, told *The Observer*: "We have grave concerns that the current freeze on housing benefit is pushing hundreds of thousands of private renters perilously close to breaking point at a time when homelessness is rising. For those hit by the freeze, housing benefit is failing to bridge the widening gap between escalating private rents and incomes that simply can't keep up.

"Whether you're a struggling family, or a young person on a low-paid zero-hours contract, in many areas of the country you'll face a grim uphill battle to keep a roof over your head and food on the table. And if you have to move, you'll find it extremely tough to find a landlord prepared to accept a rent you can afford.

"With next week's spring budget looming large, we're calling on the Government to abandon the freeze in the short term or risk making more people homeless. Ultimately, if the Government wants to cut the welfare bill in the long term, they should concentrate their efforts on building genuinely affordable homes that low earners can actually afford."

Shelter calculated the maximum amount of local housing allowance (the name for housing benefit claimed by private renters) that households would be eligible for in 2017–18, and then set this against the cost of renting in different parts of the country to establish the deficits people would face.

The alarm has also been sounded by the Local Government Association in its official submission to government ahead of the budget. It points out that the failure to build sufficient affordable homes over the last few decades has driven ever more people into expensive rented accommodation, which has to be topped up with housing benefit. When renters find they can no longer meet the costs, the local authorities are statutorily obliged to find them emergency accommodation.

The LGA submission says: "It is local government that is picking up the pieces from the long-term failure to build homes that are affordable for families… placing more families in expensive temporary accommodation [and] costing councils £3.5 billion in the last five years, rising 43% in that time."

In many parts of London the problem has reached "breaking point", according to the mayor of Hackney, Philip Glanville. In his area, the average price of a home has increased by 82% in the past five years, with rises higher than anywhere in the country in the past 20 years. Private rent now averages £1,800 a month for a two-bedroom flat, a 34% increase since 2011. Shelter calculates that in Hackney, families renting a two-bedroom home and claiming housing benefit will face a shortfall of £383.51 a month in 2017/18 as a result of rent rises and benefit freezes.

Glanville said: "This means there will be more people who cannot find the extra and who are at risk of being evicted. People assume that it is the unemployed who end up in emergency accommodation but it is so much broader than that. We are finding it is people who are in work, who are striving and in key jobs, such as teachers, nurses and trainee police officers. I don't know how the government expects people to go out to work, take their children to school and then return to one room."

Today, in a letter to *The Observer*, the heads of 15 charities and other organisations representing vulnerable people with mental health and other conditions that mean they live in "supported housing" – whose rental costs are currently covered by housing benefit – voice their concern about the impact of proposed cuts on the most needy.

"Such housing provides safe and independent long- or short-term support for people with learning disabilities, women and children escaping domestic violence, older people, people living with mental illness, people who are homeless and others," they say.

"Until now, they could rely on housing benefit to cover their rent and some service charges. Yet, under government plans, their benefit will be capped by an arbitrary formula and most will need a top-up from their local authority to fund this crucial help. As local councils already face vast budget cuts, this will cause

problems and uncertainty. The current funding system is not perfect, but the proposed system jeopardises the well-being and safety of many vulnerable people – the human and financial costs could be great.

"This can only spell bad news for our NHS, care and other public services left to pick up the pieces. We urge the Government to give the people who rely on supported housing a guarantee that they can access this housing in the future. This requires a new fair funding system that recognises the higher cost of this housing and is built on the actual needs of vulnerable people."

Jon Sparkes, chief executive of Crisis, said: "Homelessness in England has risen for the sixth year running, while temporary accommodation and B&B placements are up 52% and 250% respectively since 2009/10.

"We need housing benefit that actually covers the cost of renting, a stronger focus on preventing homelessness, and more support made available to homeless people trying to find a home to rent. At the same time, we need decisive action to make renting more accessible and affordable, along with radical solutions to tackle the severe shortage of truly affordable homes."

The Department for Work and Pensions said: "The changes to housing benefit are restoring fairness and ensuring there are no perverse disincentives that trap people on benefits. But we understand that there are some people who will need additional support. That is why we are providing £870 million in discretionary housing payments to support those who need it the most. Even with the reforms, we continue to spend £24 billion a year on housing benefit."

5 March 2017

⇨ The above information is reprinted with kind permission from *The Guardian*. Please visit www.theguardian.com for further information.

Rough sleeping statistics autumn 2017, England (revised)

This is an extract from a report by GovUK.

This publication provides information on the single night snapshot of rough sleeping that is taken annually in England using street counts and intelligence-driven estimates.

⇨ The autumn 2017 total number of rough sleepers counted and estimated was 4,751.

⇨ That was up 617, or 15% from the autumn 2016 total of 4,134.

⇨ The number of rough sleepers increased by 173, or 18% in London and 444 or 14% in the rest of England since autumn 2016.

⇨ London represented 24% of the England total rough sleepers in autumn 2017. This is up from 23% of the England total in autumn 2016.

⇨ 14% of rough sleepers were women, 20% were non-UK nationals and 8% were under 25 years old.

Rough sleeping

Local authorities' counts and estimates show that 4,751 people slept rough in England on a snapshot night in autumn 2017. This is up 617 (15%) from the autumn 2016 total of 4,134.

Of these, there were 1,137 rough sleepers in London. This is an increase of 18% from the 2016 figure of 964. In 2017, London accounted for 24% of the total England figure, compared to 23% in 2016 and 26% in 2015.

Within London, there are rough sleeping communities that move around boroughs. This leads to larger across borough movements in numbers than the change across London as a whole. Across the 33 boroughs of London 19 or 58% of local authorities reported increases, 11 or 33% reported decreases and three or 9% reported no change in the

Table 1: Rough Sleeping counts and estimates for England, London and Rest of England, 2010 to 2017

	England	% change on previous year	London	% change on previous year	Rest of England	% change on previous year
2010	1,768		415		1,353	
2011	2,181	23%	446	7%	1,735	28%
2012	2,309	6%	557	25%	1,752	1%
2013	2,414	5%	543	-3%	1,871	7%
2014	2,744	14%	742	37%	2,002	7%
2015	3,569	30%	940	27%	2,629	31%
2016	4,134	16%	964	3%	3,170	21%
2017	4,751	15%	1,137	18%	3,614	14%

Source: GovUK

number of rough sleepers since 2016. Camden reported the largest increase from 17 in 2016 to 127 this year. Westminster showed the greatest decrease of 43, or 17% from last year.

There were 3,614 rough sleepers in the rest of England, an increase of 444 or 14% from the 2016 figure of 3,170. 213 or 48% of this increase was due to increases reported by eight local authorities: Brighton and Hove, Medway, Southend-on-Sea, Oxford, Tameside, Worthing, Salford and Eastbourne.

Figures for England, London and the rest of England are shown in Table 1 above.

The rate of rough sleeping per 1,000 households is 0.20 for England, 0.31 for London and 0.18 for the rest of England. This compares to 0.18 for England, 0.27 for London and 0.16 for the rest of England in 2016. The highest rates are in the City of London (7.08 per 1,000 households), Westminster – 1.78, Brighton and Hove – 1.37, Camden – 1.14, Bedford – 1.08, Luton – 1.06 and Oxford – 1.02.

The ten local authorities who had the largest number of rough sleepers in autumn 2017 are shown in table 2 below.

Table 2: Top ten highest local authority rough sleeping counts and estimates, for England, autumn 2017

Local Authority	Total	Total autumn 2016 (% change since 2016)	Rate per 1,000 households (England average = 0.20)
Westminster	217	260 *(-17%)*	1.78
Brighton and Hove	178	144 *(24%)*	1.37
Camden	127	17 *(647%)*	1.14
Manchester	94	78 *(21%)*	0.42
Luton	87	76 *(14%)*	1.06
Bristol	86	74 *(16%)*	0.44
Bedford	76	59 *(29%)*	1.08
Newham	76	41 *(85%)*	0.62
Southend-on-sea	72	44 *(64%)*	0.91
Cornwall	68	99 *(-31%)*	0.28

Source: GovUK

Gender of rough sleepers in London and rest of England, 2017

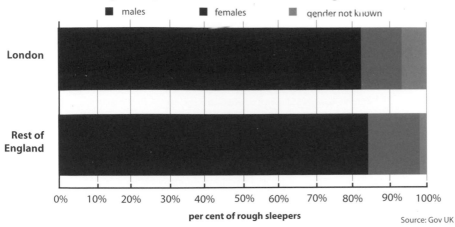

■ males   ■ females   ■ gender not known

London

Rest of England

0%   10%   20%   30%   40%   50%   60%   70%   80%   90%   100%

per cent of rough sleepers

Source: Gov UK

Age of rough sleepers in London and rest of England, 2017

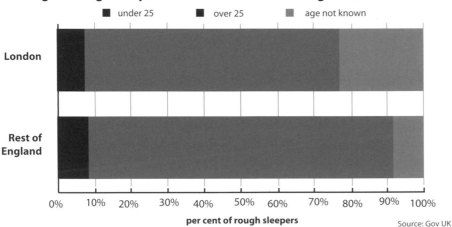

■ under 25   ■ over 25   ■ age not known

London

Rest of England

0%   10%   20%   30%   40%   50%   60%   70%   80%   90%   100%

per cent of rough sleepers

Source: Gov UK

Demographics

The below demographic figures were collected mainly through the estimates which typically included a meeting with other agencies where agreements were made about who locally was out on the streets on an agreed night. These agencies will have good knowledge on the details of the local rough sleeping population including demographics.

Of the 4,751 rough sleepers counted in autumn 2017.

⇨ 653 (14%) were women

⇨ 760 (16%) were EU nationals from outside the UK

⇨ 193 (4%) were from outside the EU.

⇨ Nationality of 402 people (8%) was not known – it suggests that some people may not wish to disclose their non-UK nationality.

⇨ 366 (8%) were 18–25 years old.

⇨ Three persons, or less than 0.1% of the England total, were under 18 years old.

The proportions of rough sleepers who were male, and who were aged under 25, were slightly lower in London than in the rest of England. However, London also had higher proportions of unknown gender and age. The proportions of rough sleepers from the EU (outside the UK) and from outside the EU were much higher in London than in the rest of England. The proportion of unknown nationality was also higher in London.

Related information for London: Combined Homelessness and Information Network (CHAIN)

The Combined Homelessness and Information Network (CHAIN) is a multi-agency database recording information about people seen rough sleeping by outreach teams in London. CHAIN is used by people working with rough sleepers in London and is managed by St Mungo's, a London-based homeless charity. Information is recorded onto the CHAIN database by people who work directly with rough sleepers in London (e.g. workers in outreach teams, day centres, hostels and resettlement teams). CHAIN does not cover 'hidden homeless' groups, such as those who are squatting or staying in places which are inaccessible to outreach workers.

The latest CHAIN financial year report, published in June 2017, shows that a total of 8,108 people were seen rough sleeping by outreach workers in London during 2016–17, virtually unchanged from 8,096 in 2015–16.

The CHAIN data is not comparable to the single night snapshot counts and estimates presented by this release, as it is a count of all individuals who were seen sleeping rough on the streets of London on at least one night during the year between 1 April 2016 and 31 March 2017. In addition it relates to an earlier time period than the autumn 2017 figures in this release. The CHAIN figure shows 8,108 rough sleepers during the whole year 2016–17, whereas the London single night snapshot gives a figure of 1,137 for autumn 2017.

The CHAIN database records identifying and demographic information about rough sleepers. Their 2016–17 report shows that:

⇨ 63% of rough sleepers were new, meaning they were seen for the first time in 2016–17,

⇨ 24% of 2016–17 rough sleepers had also been seen in 2015–16 and

⇨ 13% were returning after not having been seen during 2015–16.

Of the total recorded rough sleepers for 2016–17, 59% were seen rough sleeping only once during the year, while 5% were seen rough sleeping more than ten times during the year. Of the new rough sleepers, 72% were seen only once in the year.

The proportion of all recorded rough sleepers who were female was 15%, while 9% were aged 25 or under and 11% were aged over 55. Of the rough sleepers for whom nationality information was available, 47% were recorded as having United Kingdom as their nationality, while 30% were from Central and Eastern European countries that joined the EU in 2004 or 2007.

Of those rough sleepers who had a support needs assessment recorded, 44% had alcohol support needs, 35% drug support needs and 47% mental health support needs, with 14% having all three needs and 23% having none of these three needs. No support needs assessment was recorded for 32% of rough sleepers.

Definitions

Rough sleepers: are defined as follows for the purposes of rough sleeping counts and estimates:

People sleeping, about to bed down (sitting on/in or standing next to their bedding) or actually bedded down in the open air (such as on the streets, in tents, doorways, parks, bus shelters or encampments). People in buildings or other places not designed for habitation (such as stairwells, barns, sheds, car parks, cars, derelict boats, stations, or 'bashes' which are makeshift shelters, often comprised of cardboard boxes).

The definition does not include people in hostels or shelters, people in campsites or other sites used for recreational purposes or organised protest, squatters or travellers.

Bedded down: is taken to mean either lying down or sleeping. About to bed down includes those who are sitting in/on or near a sleeping bag or other bedding.

16 February 2018

⇨   The above extract is reprinted with kind permission from Ministry of Housing, Communities and Local Government. Please visit www. gov.uk for further information.

Number of homeless children in temporary accommodation soars 37%

Since 2014 the number of homeless children has increased by over 30k.

By Stephen Hopkins

Councils across England are housing the equivalent of an extra secondary school of pupils per month as the number of homeless children in temporary accommodation soars, according to local government leaders.

The Local Government Association (LGA) said councils are providing temporary housing for around 120,540 children with their families – a net increase of 32,650 or 37% since the second quarter of 2014.

It said the increase equates to an average of 906 extra children every month.

The LGA said placements in temporary accommodation can present serious challenges for families, from parents' employment and health to children's ability to focus on school studies and form friendships.

The LGA, which represents 350 councils across England, said the extra demand is increasing the pressure on local government.

It said councils need to be able to build more "genuinely affordable" homes and provide the support that reduces the risk of homelessness.

This means councils being able to borrow to build and to keep 100% of the receipts of any home they sell to reinvest in new and existing housing, the LGA said.

Council leaders are also calling for access to funding to provide settled accommodation for families that become homeless.

Martin Tett, the LGA's housing spokesman, said: "When councils are having to house the equivalent of an extra secondary school's worth of pupils every month, and the net cost for councils of funding for temporary accommodation has tripled in the last three years, it's clear the current situation is unsustainable for councils, and disruptive for families.

"Councils are working hard to tackle homelessness, with some truly innovative work around the country – and we now need the Government to support this local effort by allowing councils to invest in building genuinely affordable homes, and taking steps

to adapt welfare reforms to ensure housing remains affordable for low-income families."

The LGA analysed figures from the Department for Communities and Local Government (DCLG) for its findings.

A DCLG spokesman said the Government is investing £550 million to help tackle the issue, adding: "The number of children living in temporary accommodation is down from its peak in 2006, but any increase in the number of homeless families is always a concern.

"We're clear that whilst temporary accommodation is vital in making sure that no family is without a roof over their head, councils have a responsibility to find secure, good quality accommodation as quickly as possible.

"The new Homelessness Reduction Act will also help individuals and families get the help they need earlier, stopping them becoming homeless in the first place."

Anne Baxendale, director of campaigns and policy at Shelter, said: "Every day we speak to families desperate to escape the dingy, cramped hostel room they're forced to live in, for weeks if not months, as overstretched councils can't find them anywhere else. The situation is getting worse as the lack of affordable homes and welfare cuts bite deeper.

"The Government has the tools to break this cycle of heartache and homelessness. Firstly, they must abandon the freeze on housing benefit that's denying thousands of families the essential top-up needed to pay for rising rents. And, in the longer term, they must build decent homes that families on lower incomes can actually afford to live in."

22 July 2017

⇨ The above information is reprinted with kind permission from The Huffington Post UK. Please visit www.huffingtonpost.co.uk for further information.

Number of rough sleepers up by 134% as Tories accused of "light touch" approach to tackling homelessness

Government condemned for failing to tackle crisis as figures show 73 per cent more children are homeless than in 2010.

By May Bulman

The number of rough sleepers in the UK has soared by 134 per cent since the Tories took power, new figures show, prompting accusations from the Government spending watchdog that ministers have failed to tackle the problem.

A damning report by the National Audit Office (NAO) revealed that there had been a 60 per cent rise in households in temporary accommodation over the last six years, affecting 120,540 children – 73 per cent more youngsters than were made homeless in March 2011.

An autumn snapshot survey last year recorded 4,134 rough sleepers – marking an increase of 134 per cent since the Tory-led coalition took power in 2010 – while the number of homeless families approaching councils and being assessed as entitled to temporary accommodation rose by 48 per cent to 59,090.

Despite the worsening crisis – branded a "national scandal" by opposition MPs – the Government has continued with a "light touch" approach that cannot be considered value for money, according to the report.

All forms of homelessness have increased "significantly" and are costing more than £1 billion a year to deal with, the NAO states, with the ending of private sector tenancies having become the main cause of homelessness in England, showing a threefold increase in numbers since 2010/11.

Government measures are believed to have exacerbated the problem, with the report stating that local housing allowance reforms are "likely to have contributed" to making tenancies for claimants less affordable and "are an element of the increase in homelessness".

Rents have gone up at the same time as household incomes from benefits have been cut, with rent costs across England up by three times as much as wages, except in the North and the East Midlands.

In an indication of the soaring renting costs in the capital, private sector rents in London have gone up by 24 per cent since 2010 – eight times the average rise in earnings.

Local councils have had to foot the bill for the soaring levels of homelessness, with most of the £1.1 billion spent on housing people in 2015/16 going on temporary accommodation, up by 39 per cent in real terms since 2010/11 – from £606 million to £845 million.

Alarmingly, over the same period, spending on other services, such as prevention, support and administration, fell by nine per cent – from £334 million to £303 million.

The NAO found nine in ten households in temporary accommodation that have been housed outside their council area were placed there by a London authority, with councils in the capital buying up properties in towns such as Bexley, Luton and Medway to house homeless families.

The report states: "It appears likely that the decrease in affordability of properties in the private rented sector, of which welfare reforms such as the capping of local housing allowance are an element, have driven this increase in homelessness.

"Despite this, the Government has not evaluated the impact of its welfare reforms on homelessness, or the impact of the mitigations that it has put in place."

Responding to the findings, shadow secretary of state for housing John Healey said the report should "shame" the Government, and claimed government policy decisions were "directly responsible" for the rise in homelessness under the Tories.

"This report from the Government's spending watchdog should shame ministers. When this Government fails, rising homelessness will be on its political tombstone. The increase in homelessness since 2010 is visible in almost every town and city in the country but today's report shows ministers haven't even bothered to draw up a proper plan to deal with it," he said.

"After an unprecedented decline in homelessness under Labour, government policy decisions are directly responsible for the rise in homelessness. You can't help the homeless without the homes, and ministers have driven new affordable house building to a 24-year low."

Labour's Meg Hillier, who chairs the Public Accounts Committee, said: "It is a national scandal that more and more people are made homeless every year. This report illustrates the very real human cost of the Government's failure to ensure people have access to affordable housing.

"The Department for Communities and local government's 'light touch' approach clearly isn't working. Its

plans for the future merely seem to shift more responsibility and cost to local authorities at a time when they are already stretched."

Shedding light on the burden the homelessness issue is putting on local authorities, the Local Government Association's housing spokesman Cllr Martin Tett said: "Homelessness is a tragedy, as a settled home is crucial to health and well-being for individuals and families, and is a central cornerstone of successful communities.

"Rising homelessness is a huge challenge for councils, which are having to house the equivalent of an extra secondary school's worth of homeless children in temporary accommodation every month. The net cost to councils of doing this has tripled in the last three years, as they plug the gap between rising rents and frozen housing benefit.

"Councils are working hard to tackle homelessness and are focusing on preventing it happening. We now need the Government to support this local effort, by allowing councils to invest in building genuinely affordable homes and providing the support and resources they need to help prevent people becoming homeless in the first place."

Polly Neate, chief executive of homeless charity Shelter, called for a "whole new approach" to the way homes are built so that developers' profits are not prioritised above the needs of homeless people.

"Every rise in house prices is bad news for millions of families struggling to find a home of their own. And this will continue to be the case so long as we have a house building system that puts big developers' profits above people," she said.

"The only way to bring house prices back within reach of ordinary people is to take a whole new approach to the way we build homes, which drastically reduces the cost of land."

Auditor general Sir Amyas Morse accused the Government of leaving

"gaps" in its approach to homelessness, saying it had failed to evaluate the impact of its housing reforms.

"Homelessness in all its forms has significantly increased in recent years, driven by several factors. Despite this, the Government has not evaluated the impact of its reforms on this issue, and there remain gaps in its approach," he said.

"It is difficult to understand why the department persisted with its light touch approach in the face of such a visibly growing problem. Its recent performance in reducing homelessness therefore cannot be considered value for money."

A Government spokesperson said: "Tackling homelessness is a complex issue with no single solution, but this Government is determined to help the most vulnerable in society, make sure people always have a roof over their head.

"That is why we are investing £550 million to 2020 to address the issue and implementing the most ambitious legislative reform in decades, the Homelessness Reduction Act. This act will ensure that more people get the help they need earlier to prevent them from becoming homeless in the first place.

"This Government is committed to ensuring people always have a roof over their heads which is why we've committed to eliminating rough sleeping entirely. There's more to do and ministers will set out plans shortly."

12 September 2017

⇨ The above information is reprinted with kind permission from *The Independent*. Please visit www.independent.co.uk for further information.

Poverty, evictions and forced moves

This is an extract from the above report.

There has been a rapid increase in evictions over the past 12 years, and especially of 'no fault' evictions from the private rented sector. This project explores why this has occurred, and the impact these have had on the lives of tenants who lose their homes.

This Findings report was updated on 3 August 2017 to use updated and backdated data from the Ministry of Justice bulletin 'Mortgage and Landlords Possession Statistics in England and Wales'.

By Anna Clarke, Charlotte Hamilton, Michael Jones and Kathryn Muir

Key points

⇨ In the past 12 years, the rented sector as a whole has grown by a third, and the number of tenants being evicted from their homes has grown by a fifth: 7,200 more tenants lost their homes in 2015 than in 2003.

⇨ The number of tenants evicted by private landlords exceeded the number evicted by social landlords for the first time in 2014.

⇨ The increase in repossessions in recent years has been almost entirely due to the increasing use of 'no fault' evictions, using Section 21 (S21) of the Housing Act 1988, which enables landlords to end an assured shorthold tenancy after the end of its fixed term, with two months' notice, without giving any reason. Tenants do not have a defence against a valid S21 notice.

⇨ The use of S21 is highly concentrated geographically. Four out of every five repossessions using S21 are in London, the East and the South East, and nearly two-thirds are in London alone, although London only has one-fifth of the private rented housing stock. Even within London, repossessions using S21 are highly concentrated, with a third occurring in only five boroughs.

⇨ Changes in welfare benefits have combined to make rents unaffordable to benefit claimants in many areas.

⇨ As a result, tenants on low incomes are being evicted because their benefits do not pay market rents, and they are unable to afford alternative homes in the private rented sector, or access social housing.

Background

Over 40,000 tenants were evicted from their homes by landlords in 2015, and many more felt forced to move from their homes due to problems of affordability, the condition of the property, or disputes with their landlord.

The loss of a home can be a traumatic and challenging experience for anyone, and for tenants with limited financial resources this can add to other difficulties that they experience.

"With the £50 per month (Housing Benefit shortfall) coming out of the JSA – that's almost a week's money in itself – and then you've got the other bills… I just couldn't make it work. I had to choose, what do I pay this month – do I pay the rent? Do I pay the electricity? Do I buy some food? And it just snowballed."

Single man, 40s

The aim of the research was to understand the factors that prompt evictions and forced moves, the tenants who are affected, how these have changed over time, and what could be done to avoid such events. The focus was primarily on England, and

interviewees were recruited via Shelter housing offices in Bournemouth, Bristol, Colchester, Hackney (covering the whole of London), Manchester, and Slough: areas selected because they had high and/or increasing numbers of evictions.

Context and trends in evictions

Social housing tenants can usually only be evicted for rent arrears or a breach of tenancy, such as anti-social behaviour (ASB). In contrast, most tenants in the private rented sector have assured shorthold tenancies (ASTs), which can also be ended after their initial fixed term without the landlord having to give a reason ('no fault' evictions, often known as Section 21 evictions, under Section 21 of the Housing Act 1988), or with two months' notice thereafter.

Historically, social housing landlords have evicted tenants at a higher rate than private sector landlords but the rate of repossession per thousand tenancies in the social housing sector has been in decline since 2003, while the rate per thousand in the private rented sector (PRS) has been increasing. The rate of repossessions in the two sectors is now similar, at 4.7 tenants per thousand per annum.

Over four-fifths of the increase in repossessions in recent years has been due to the increasing use of 'no fault' evictions, using Section 21, but the use of S21 is highly concentrated geographically. Four out of every five (81%) of all repossessions using S21 are in London, the East and the South East, and nearly two-thirds (62%) are in London alone, although London only has one-fifth (21%) of the private rented housing stock. Even within London, repossessions using S21 are highly concentrated, with a third of S21 evictions occurring in only five boroughs.

What are the causes of forced moves and evictions?

This research sought to understand both the structural factors that affect eviction rates, and individual factors that make some people vulnerable. National data from the English Housing Survey suggests that just under a quarter of current tenants reported that their last move from private rented properties in England were forced in some way – rather than because the tenant wanted to move.

The cumulative impact of freezing Local Housing Allowance (LHA) or permitting only below-inflation increases has been that it now lags significantly below the 30th percentile of market rents to which it is in principle linked. Outside London, average monthly shortfalls range from £22 to £70 per month, whereas in central London average shortfalls range from £124 to £1,036 per month. The shortfall between the LHA rate and the 30th percentile rent means that tenants in receipt of Housing Benefit are either squeezed into the bottom end of the market, or are forced to make up the difference from other income.

Findings from the interviews – the causes of forced moves and evictions

The research highlighted the issues around living in, and leaving, properties at the lower end of the PRS.

The experiences were characterised by poverty, lower-quality housing and poor landlord behaviour.

Finding any housing at all that evicted tenants could afford was virtually impossible.

The majority of tenants in the PRS were being evicted under S21, though in some cases they were aware of this having resulted from rent arrears, a rent that had fallen below market rates, the landlord wanting to sell up, or suspected retaliation by landlords after complaints had been made. It was apparent that the legislation designed to protect tenants from revenge evictions was failing to cover many situations. In the social sector, rent arrears and breaches of tenancy were more common reasons.

"I asked the landlord, repeatedly, to fix these things – in the end, he served me a notice of eviction."

Single man, 40s

A variety of factors had caused rent arrears. Problems with Housing Benefit and/or other benefits were the most common, followed by changes in circumstances meaning that what had previously been affordable had become unaffordable. Some tenants had had benefits sanctioned and Housing Benefit stopped as a result, causing arrears to mount quickly. In a few cases, tenancies had been taken on that would never have been affordable. Some tenants had failed to pay their rent, even with adequate income, often related to mental health difficulties.

Forced moves were rare, as the majority of tenants held onto anything they could manage, including very unfit housing and with landlords who were harassing them, because they could not find anywhere else to live.

The experiences of forced moves and evictions

Eviction proceedings could be protracted. Whilst this did buy people time to look for somewhere else, it also placed households in extreme levels of stress. Some were trying hard to find a new home, but found there was nothing they could afford. Others waited anxiously for the eviction,

hoping the local authority would then assist them. Agency fees, the need for a guarantor, and finding a deposit, were all major barriers to finding a new home. Most tenants would prefer social housing, but were either ineligible, or not a sufficient priority to be allocated it. Some tenants had lost their home and were living in temporary accommodation, which was overcrowded and stressful. Sharing facilities with difficult housemates was also problematic.

"It's all of us in one room, you can imagine the tension… everyone's snapping because they don't have their own personal space… it's just a room with two beds. My little brother has to do his homework on the floor."

Woman, under 21

Some people had found their own informal housing arrangements, but this could involve putting their hosts' tenancies at risk for accommodating them. Several of those who had lost homes had done so as a result of accommodating a homeless friend or family member. Ten of the interviewees were street homeless, half of whom had moved directly from a tenancy with a landlord to being on the street. Living on the street posed huge day-to-day difficulties, making it very hard to secure new housing.

Conclusions

Housing Benefit is no longer a safety net for low-income households in many parts of the country. LHA rates were insufficient to enable low-income households to find alternative accommodation if they lost their home, and landlords in high-pressure markets were refusing benefit claimants, causing homelessness. The lower end of the PRS is under pressure from the competing political agendas of reducing Housing Benefit costs and driving out poor practice in the PRS, resulting in a squeeze on low-income tenants.

The experience of forced moves and evictions were extremely stressful for low-income households as they struggled to find alternative homes. In a housing shortage, landlords can choose who they want as tenants.

Increasing eviction rates are linked to the overall growth of the PRS and to cuts to LHA. Whilst the greatest impact is being felt in London, similar issues were found in other high-pressure markets. The continuing programme of cuts and restraints on state assistance with housing costs will intensify this pressure.

3 August 2017

⇨ The above extract is reprinted with kind permission from the Joseph Rowntree Foundation. Please visit www.jfr.org.uk for further information.

Hidden homelessness: an avoidable tragedy

Homelessness finally appears to be rising up the political agenda.

By Sara Gariban

New figures released by the charity Crisis show that the number of 'hidden' homeless will rise by 47% to 13,400 over the next decade, unless the gGvernment takes immediate action.

As the term suggests, the 'hidden' homeless are not the rough sleepers you may see in your town or city. This group do not always appear in statistics or present at the usual services. They do not have access to suitable, fixed accommodation, but use a range of informal means to avoid sleeping on the streets on a permanent basis. This can mean staying on a friend or relative's sofa and hopping from place to place.

Homelessness finally appears to be rising up the political agenda, with the introduction of Housing First pilot schemes and the launch of the Homelessness Reduction Taskforce.

Unfortunately, wider decisions in different areas of housing policy have combined to create a cascade of failure, pushing people into this insecure, unsettling existence. Hidden homelessness will remain a growing problem until the Government addresses its root causes in the structural problems in the housing market.

Firstly, years of undersupply have made social housing an unattainable prospect for most. In the 1980s, nearly three quarters of non home-owners lived in social rented accommodation. Reflecting a downturn in investment, that proportion is now less than half and, since 2010/11, the number of new social homes built or bought has continued to drop from 39,560 to 6,550 in 2015/16. The waiting list now stands at 1.2 million.

New policies stand to exacerbate, rather than relieve, the problem. The Welfare Reform and Work Act (2016) requires social landlords to reduce their rents by one per cent. This has hit their budgets, discouraging investment in new social housing stock. As a result, the Office for Budget Responsibility estimates that 14,000 fewer social homes will be built between now and 2020/21.

With insufficient social housing to provide a safety net for the majority of people, those who are 'just about managing' are being pushed towards the private rented sector (PRS).

Private Rented Sector: unaffordable

But the PRS is itself dominated by high rents and insecure tenures. One

in seven tenants privately renting from a landlord is paying more than half of their income in rent. Private renters already tend to be the young and those on the lowest incomes, who already face financial insecurity. Burdensome rents mean that 1.3 million households are left below the Joseph Rowntree Foundation Minimum Income Standard after paying rent. This huge financial burden is, for many, an insurmountable barrier to saving for home ownership. In addition, fluctuations in income can put tenants at real risk of losing their home and being forced out.

Even tenants who can pay their rent are not safe. Government data shows that the end of an Assured Shorthold Tenancy has become the leading cause of homelessness over the last decade. Specifically, research by Shelter has shown that, since 2011, the rise in the number of households evicted from a privately rented home has accounted for 78% of the rise in homelessness over the period.

As part of the autumn budget, the chancellor Philip Hammond announced a consultation on the longer term leases for renters. While this demonstrates a commitment to exploring the issue of insecurity, this move does not address the scale of the problem.

Years of low investment in social housing, lack of regulation of the Private Rented Sector, and the insecurity of shorthold tenancies has created a system where those who are struggling can fall too easily through the cracks.

That's why the Government must take comprehensive action to tackle this toxic combination of factors together – and end the damaging limbo of hidden homelessness.

25 January 2018

⇨ The above extract is reprinted with kind permission from Politics. co.uk. Please visit www.politics. co.uk for futher information.

© 2018 Politics. co.uk

Local government association briefing debate on the availability and affordability of housing, House of Lords

Key messages

⇨ The nation is facing a housing crisis. Dealing with the crisis is vital if we are to ensure that all residents are able to benefit from economic growth. Everyone needs a home that is affordable, good quality and is well-supported by local services and infrastructure. Councils must be part of the solution to providing more homes in the right places.

⇨ The country needs to build 250,000 homes a year to keep up with demand. The last time housebuilding reached this level, in the 1970s, local government built around 40 per cent of them. Bold new action is needed to solve our housing crisis and a renaissance in house building by councils must be at the heart of this.

⇨ Ahead of the autumn budget we are calling on the Government to re-establish self-financing from 2020, lift the housing borrowing cap, and to provide a sustainable long-term financial framework for councils to invest in new homes, of all tenures, through Housing Revenue Accounts (HRA).

⇨ In most areas the rise in rents and house prices above earnings makes housing less affordable for a large and growing proportion of the population. The LGA has found that one in seven private renters spends over half their income on rent.

⇨ Councils are working with communities to approve nine in ten planning applications. A new wave of affordable housing must now be built, linked to a new definition of affordable housing as costing 30 per cent of household income or less.

⇨ The Government must act now to end rising homelessness by lifting the Local Housing Allowance (LHA) freeze and exempting temporary accommodation from the overall benefit cap.

Availability of housing

The housing crisis is having a significant impact on our communities and economies. It affects everyone from the young families unable to get on the property ladder, to the older people who want to downsize but can't find the specialist housing they need, to the people who find themselves on the streets or in temporary accommodation.

Local government shares the collective national ambition to increase housing supply but housebuilding is currently well below the levels required for a fully functioning housing market. Last year housing supply increased by 190,000 new homes, but we need to be building 300,000 homes before they become affordable.[1] The last time the country built more than 250,000 homes in a year, in the 1970s, local

---

1 National Audit Office report, *Housing in England: overview*, January 2017

government built around 40 per cent of them. Local authorities are approving nine out of ten planning applications, and are using all the tools currently at their disposal to build more homes, alongside the vital infrastructure and services that sustain communities.

It is good that the Government has accepted our argument that councils must be part of the solution to our chronic housing shortage, and we were pleased to see additional funding for affordable homes announced by the Prime Minister. Bold new action is needed to solve our housing crisis and councils are well placed to bridge the gap between housing need and building rates. As our Housing Commission[2] has highlighted, investment in housing has significant wider benefits for communities and the right homes in the right places can boost employment, improve well-being and support an ageing population.

Councils need financial flexibilities and a sustainable long-term financial framework to invest in new homes, of all tenures, through Housing Revenue Accounts and other ventures. The Government should work to remove housing for borrowing investment from contributing to public sector debt, and allow the Housing Revenue Account (HRA) borrowing cap to be lifted. Councils also need the ability to retain 100 per cent of Right to Buy receipts to rapidly build new affordable homes.

We are calling on the Government to commit to no further increases in the new homes bonus (NHB) threshold for any council. The potential for future unexpected increases in the threshold is a concern for councils. A commitment to no further increases for any council would provide much-needed certainty. In the longer term, the overall level of resourcing for

council investment in housing and infrastructure, including the new homes bonus, should be reviewed to ensure an appropriate balance of funding and incentive in all areas.

Affordability of housing

In most areas the rise in house prices above earnings has made housing less affordable for a large and growing proportion of the population. For many households, high housing costs means cutting back on other outgoings, squeezing into smaller properties, or moving out of the area where they have built lives for themselves and their families.

For government, it means greater pressure on housing benefit spending which is now well over £20 billion a year, accounting for 80 per cent of all public investment in housing.[3] Last year the country built around 30,000 new affordable homes, the lowest number in 24 years, with many being priced at levels not affordable for many families.[4]

Rising rents make it increasingly difficult to buy a first home. Analysis from the LGA has revealed that one in seven private renters (14%) now spend more than half of their total income on rent.[5] For house buyers, interest rates on mortgages have rarely been lower, but escalating house prices mean average deposits for first time buyers are now costing 71 per cent of annual income. Young people today are half as likely to be on the housing ladder as 20 years ago.[6]

Their chances of ownership are increasingly determined by how fortunate their parents were in previous housing booms.

Only an increase of all types of housing – including those for affordable or social rent – will solve our housing shortage and a renaissance in house building by councils is ultimately needed if we are to make housing affordable for future generations. This is the best way to reduce waiting lists and housing benefit, keep rents low and help more people get on the housing ladder. To help achieve this, councils want the Government to commit to building a new wave of different affordable housing options linked to a new definition of affordable housing as being of a cost that is 30 per cent of household income or less.

Homelessness

Homelessness is increasing. Loss of tenancy now triggers a third of all new homelessness cases, as rents rise and reduced welfare assistance limits landlords' capacity to provide for low-income households. The last six years have seen a 44 per cent increase in the number of homeless households and a 102 per cent increase in rough sleeping. Councils are currently housing 75,740 families including 118,960 children in temporary accommodation, at a net cost that has tripled in the last three years.[7]

Despite overall growing rates of homelessness, local government is increasingly successful in preventing it. In 2015/16 more than 90 per cent of households helped by councils had their homelessness prevented.[8] However councils cannot tackle rising homelessness on their own, particularly as people most vulnerable to homelessness often need access to other services to overcome

---

2 'Building our homes, communities and future: preliminary findings from the LGA Housing Commission', June 2016

3 UK Housing Review, Chartered Institute of Housing, 2016

4 Live tables on affordable housing supply, DCLG, 2017

5 LGA analysis published July 2017, based on the Labour Force Survey, the Valuations Office Agency Private Rental Market statistics and the English Housing Survey.

6 Building our homes, communities and future, LGA, 2016

7 Live tables on homelessness, DCLG, 2017

8 Live tables on homelessness, DCLG, 2017

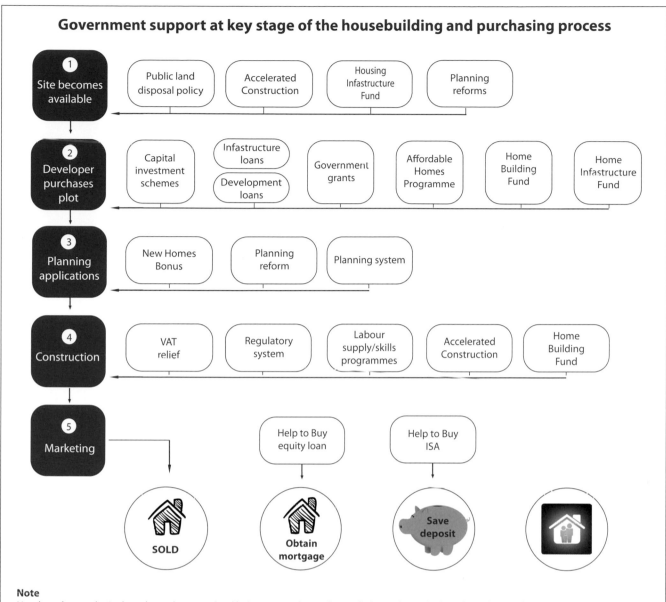

Government support at key stage of the housebuilding and purchasing process

Note
Numbered steps depict key phases between land being put on the market and a home being built and purchased. The measures associated with each phase are designed to provide financial incentives to developers to accelerate their building plans, or help overcome the barriers they might face in doing so.

Source: National Audit Office

challenges, such as mental health or addiction issues.

To help end homelessness we call for the Government to make cheaper finance available to councils seeking to acquire homes for the use of homeless households at scale. Alongside this, the Government should lift the Local Housing Allowance (LHA) freeze, link the allowance to the change in rent levels, and reconsider plans to apply the LHA rate to social housing from 2019. Councils also want to see temporary accommodation exempted from the overall benefit cap.

Planning

Councils want to use the planning system to work positively with developers to build prosperous places. However, planning departments are severely under-resourced, while local taxpayers are subsidising planning services by 30 per cent because nationally set planning fees do not cover the full costs.

The Government should work towards an efficient and proactive role for planning services to deliver homes by allowing councils to set fees locally and exploring how other services can support planning services. Key to this

is rapidly progressing the commitment to allow councils to increase planning fees by 20 per cent[9] and committing to allow every council the flexibility to increase them up to 40 per cent while testing a fair and transparent scheme of local fee setting.

12 October 2017

⇨ The above extract is reprinted with kind permission from Gov. uk. Please visit www.gov.uk for further information.

© Crown copyright 2018

9 Housing White Paper, DCLG, 2017

Rough sleeper dies near busy Sainsbury's on central London street

A homeless man describes his "absolute shock" after waking up next to his dead friend.

By Steven Hopkins

A rough sleeper has told of his "absolute shock" at having been awoken by police to the news that the man sleeping beside him had died during the night.

James, who declined to give his last name, said the man in his mid-40s is thought to have died shortly after 2.15am on Tuesday morning, on a pavement outside Curry's PC World on London's busy Tottenham Court Road.

The death comes just days after around 100 rough sleepers were evicted from a disused building nearby, which had been turned into a makeshift shelter by volunteers hoping to protect the homeless community during freezing temperatures in March.

Homeless charity Crisis described the death as a "tragic reminder of the dangers faced by thousands of people who have no choice but to sleep on the streets".

Shelter said that more needed to be done to help people off the streets "and to get to grips with the root causes of homelessness itself".

As James gathered up his bedding to leave the police cordon where his friend still lay concealed by blankets, the 34-year-old described his friend's final hours.

Known as "Irish Keith", James said his friend had smoked spice – the synthetic cannabis banned under the Psychoactive Substances Act in April 2016 – before going to sleep for the night.

"Right before he died, he had walked off to get a blanket and I'd rolled (a cigarette) for him... he was too pissed to do it," James said, adding that Keith had "looked out" for him on the streets since he had become homeless two weeks ago.

"It's an absolutely shocking thing to wake up to... I thought we were been woken up (by police) to be moved on," he said.

Keith had been homeless for 27 years, was on medication, and had a cast on his leg, James said. "Apparently, on the CCTV he was seen sitting up on his elbow, and then he just fell back and that was it."

Clara, who had also been sleeping outside the Curry's store, said: "It's so scary that he's still right there."

The body, shrouded in blankets, was still visible on the pavement after the morning rush hour around 10am.

Police at the scene said there was nothing suspicious about the death which the London Ambulance Service attended at 7.55am.

James said Keith's death had given him a renewed sense of urgency to get in to accommodation: "I need to get something actionable... anything to get me off the streets."

The UK is experiencing record levels of rough sleeping with local authorities estimating there were around 4,751 rough sleepers on a single night in autumn 2017 – the highest number since comparable records began in 2010.

James said he had become homeless after losing his job as a bricklayer's assistant in Cambridge, which came with accommodation. The lay off came without warning: "They just said: 'we don't have any work for you anymore'."

Camden Outreach workers spoke to James and Clara at the scene, offering them hot drinks from a nearby cafe. One worker said they would be attempting to get James into accommodation tonight under the London Mayor Sadiq Khan's "no second night out" homeless plan.

Clara, who has been sleeping intermittently at her father's house, would be able to stay with the housing shelter Pathways.

James was relieved by the news, having earlier said he was at a loss about what to do next. He said the outcome of a tax return appointment in 13 days, on 9 April, was his only hope to afford accommodation.

Representatives from Crisis and Shelter said they were "deeply saddened" by the death.

Matthew Downie, director of policy at Crisis, said in a statement: "It is a grim reality that the average age of death for a homeless person is just 47.

"No one should have to face the dangers of the streets, but we have the evidence that rough sleeping can be ended.

"Recent progress by the Government, including the founding of its rough sleeping taskforce has come not a moment too soon. Now we must build on it, and work together to end homelessness for good."

Greg Beales, director of communications, policy and campaigns at Shelter, said: "Rough sleepers are at the sharpest end of our housing crisis and endure terrible conditions, resulting in poor health and sadly, shorter lives.

"More needs to be done to help people off the streets, and to get to grips with the root causes of homelessness itself.

"That means tackling the chronic lack of genuinely affordable homes and making sure housing benefit actually reflects the cost of renting in the short-term."

27 March 2018

⇨ The above information is reprinted with kind permission from The Huffington Post UK. Please visit www.huffingtonpost.co.uk for further information.

© 2018 Oath (UK) Limited

Night shelters rebranded: "people still think of one room, 25 beds, drugs and chaos"

Many homeless hostels have modernised, even changing their names to avoid negative stereotypes – but not all are able to provide more than basic shelter.

By Tamsin Rutter

When Glyn found himself homeless at age 51, he was almost pleased to find out he'd be spending a few weeks at Winchester Churches Nightshelter. A former officer in the Royal Signals fluent in German, he likens his new sleeping quarters to a luxurious barrack block.

Before being evicted from a shared house, Glyn used to volunteer at a drop-in centre for rough sleepers in Basingstoke, where he had heard people speak highly of Winchester's shelter – and not so highly of others. He was especially keen to avoid one Basingstoke hostel known for violence and drug-taking: "I would rather cut off my own leg than spend a night in that place," he says. He's not the only one: fellow Winchester resident Chris, 34, used to choose nights on the street over a bed in some of Hampshire's other shelters.

Glyn lost his home in the private rented sector after a psychotic outburst that happened when he stopped taking medication for post-traumatic stress disorder. "Ten days later I've got my housemate pinned to the wall with a knife against his throat," he says. "That's not me. I'm not a violent person. The worst part of it is not remembering."

But Glyn, a chef in his spare time who has just finished marinating meatballs for Winchester Churches' 17 residents, is hopeful about his future. "I have seen a lot of documentaries about homeless people in larger cities. Pretty grim places," he says. "But this is almost like a hotel. It's got everything that a person needs. It has all the people there to help you move on."

More than just shelter

When it was established in 1988, Winchester Churches Nightshelter's origins were typical to many shelters: camp beds erected in a church hall, packed away in the morning and moved on to the next hall. With no regulation on alcohol and a first come, first served policy, violence was prevalent and assistance was short-term and unfocused.

But the shelter – now a charity – has since evolved. It now has a dedicated 10-bedroom property, formerly a Victorian gasworks, which prioritises the most vulnerable and provides access to a full-time advocate, three counsellors, computer training, financial advice, cooking lessons, tenancy training, work experience and nightly breathalyser tests to ensure residents don't exceed the drink-driving limit.

Those in charge at Winchester are considering rebranding to avoid being stereotyped. "We're masses more than just a night shelter," says Michele Price, Winchester's manager. "The word 'nightshelter' has negative connotations – people still think of the old one room with 25 beds, drugs and alcohol and chaos. We have to move with the times."

It is a decision that has already been taken by other UK hostels, including Oxford Homeless Pathways (OxHoP) – previously known as Oxford Night Shelter – which changed its "old-fashioned name" because "it's a really derogatory term", according to chief executive Lesley Dewhurst.

Paul Anderson, policy manager at Homeless Link, understands why some shelters want to shed the term. He started working in night shelters a couple of decades ago when many of them still had beds lined up, dormitory-style, with at least 20 to a room. But things had begun to change. Almost 4,000 new units of accommodation were built between 1990 and 1999 under the Rough Sleepers Initiative – a response to a rise in homelessness caused by reductions to benefits, rising unemployment and the sell-off of social housing under the Thatcher Government. The scheme was supported by mental health and resettlement teams that helped rough sleepers to retain accommodation.

"There was a realisation that if you didn't run things decently people weren't going to get off the streets. That was probably the first big ideological switch," Anderson says.

The Rough Sleepers Unit set up by the Labour Government in 1997 had a more comprehensive approach, reducing homelessness by two-thirds in everywhere except London – but it wasn't until 2005 that the focus switched to the nature of night shelters themselves. The £90 million Hostels Capital Improvement Programme was born out of research into the poor quality of many homeless hostels, which had little impact on helping people move towards independent living. There was "a consensus around the need to reduce the size and configuration of hostels" and help staff to engage better with residents.

This evolved into the Places of Change programme of 2008, which continued to change the ethos and physical space in UK night shelters to "a bed for somebody and a reason for them to get out of it in the morning," says Anderson. More hostels have begun involving previously homeless people in the design and development of services, he adds, such as King Georges hostel in Westminster, London, run by the Riverside Housing Association.

But despite this progress, terminology remains a problem. On the face of it, there's little to distinguish a hostel or shelter such as Winchester – where clients come through a referral system and the emphasis is on safety and support – with those that are temporary, seasonal or emergency, says Anderson.

This has caused issues in the past. After a court ruled that a homeless hostel in Anglesey did not legally constitute a dwelling and so could not claim housing benefit on behalf of residents, local authorities elsewhere began refusing similar benefit claims. But, Anderson says, the circumstances in Anglesey were unique and many night shelters offer a nicer environment and should be considered homes; there's no logic to suspending housing benefits for other properties.

Because some people still experience fear, bed bugs and noisy, prison-like conditions, these experiences filter through to other homeless people waiting to be placed in a hostel. "I didn't expect it to be as nice as it is," says Holly, the self-appointed baby of Winchester Churches Nightshelter, who has just turned 18. "I expected it to be full of drunk alcoholics and drug abusers. It was really welcoming and made me feel safe."

Michele Price, Winchester's manager, is proud of the emphasis on safety. "I've had people who've come in from Guildford who've said, 'I drink but I like the breathalyser because it keeps me safe and I've been in Guildford where somebody's thrown a fire extinguisher through the wall and I'm blinking terrified'," she says.

"I've had one incident where I've been scared in the ten years I've been here. Oh no, two – there was somebody in the car park with an axe. But he never got very far!"

The other thing that sets Winchester apart is its size. Homeless people often have very complex needs: Glyn, pulling his life back together and searching for a job in engineering; Chris, grieving after his partner's suicide; Holly, kicked out of her dad's home and sick of dealing with children's social services; Mark, 27, constantly nervous and trembling from the pills he takes to help his psychosis. Everyone gets tailored assistance and each new resident meets the manager.

"I think where we're lucky is that we're quite small and we can't accept everyone, but we keep it safe," says Price. "And because we're quite small we get to know everyone and can provide a better service. If we trebled and had 50 to 70 people, I don't think we'd produce as good or homely a service."

Last year the shelter accepted 118 residents but turned away 422 others. There's a trend towards making homeless hostels as small as possible, says Anderson. But he adds that with homelessness rising and UK night shelters struggling through a funding crisis, this is not always possible – particularly in cities such as London, Brighton, Liverpool or Manchester.

"There's a realisation that running gigantic programmes can be problematic unless you can get the support right," he says. "In an ideal world we would run nothing more than 20 beds."

25 September 2015

⇨ The above information is reprinted with kind permission from *The Guardian*. Please visit www.theguardian.com for further information.

'Buy a homeless' project participants explain why they're happy to be 'sold'

Is it really as controversial as it sounds?

By Sarah Ann Harris and Eve Hartley

Selling homeless people and fitting them with tracking devices sounds pretty controversial. So when I find myself walking into an old courtroom (now a function room in a Covent Garden restaurant) where the 'sale' of two rough sleepers is being announced, I have a lot of questions.

The room is empty save for the artist himself, a PR and a burly security guard. It's awkward – no one really seems sure of the correct social protocol for such an event. At last, the homeless people troop in and proceedings commence.

This is the Hornsleth Homeless Tracker project.

Kristian von Hornsleth, a Danish artist, is facilitating the 'sale' of 10 homeless people. The group will be 'purchased' by buyers and given tracking devices. Their 'owners' will then have access to an exclusive app where they can track them wherever they go. Hornsleth describes it as being like a "real life Tamagotchi". The buyers will also receive a gold-plated picture of their homeless person.

Although this whole project is being done under the guise of performance art, it has – quite understandably – provoked criticism and outrage. But the men being 'sold' are sceptical of claims that they are being exploited.

Darren O'Shea, who has been homeless for three years after the effects of PTSD saw his marriage break down, tells me: "We get criticised and abused every day anyway. But if this is drawing people's attention then it can't be a bad thing.

"Just walk around Piccadilly and Leicester Square and up Shaftesbury Avenue and count how many homeless people you walk past. I guarantee there won't be less than 20. That's just not right. How does that happen? With all these adverts on telly, 'give to homeless charities' and obviously it doesn't get to us because we're still there. They say it's all admin costs, admin fees but homelessness is increasing year-on-year.

"Nothing else has worked. Every Christmas you get the Salvation Army with their adverts on telly every year, nothing changes. If it has to shock people into doing something about it, go for it."

"It's more dangerous sleeping on the streets"

Darren O'Shea, 'purchased' homeless man

When asked if he thinks the project is dehumanising, O'Shea says: "Not really. I'm a dot on the screen doing what I do every day anyway. It's only

one person who can see where I was an hour ago, it's not as if he can actually come and track me down."

Does he not find the idea of someone knowing his movement unnerving?

"Not really. It's more dangerous sleeping on the streets."

Hornsleth announces the 'sale' of two of the men, who are required to sign contracts. Then he asks the rest of the group up to the judge's bench and tips a pile of cash – £20,000 in used bank notes – onto the desk. This is their share of the profits, which they will receive in a year's time if they stick to the rules. The artist invites them to touch the cash and "smell it", before getting them to pose with it. I get the feeling Hornsleth is really hamming up his role. He seems to take great pleasure in telling the group he is off on holiday to Tuscany, playing the panto villain. Many of the participants jokingly put wads in their pockets, though all the money is returned by the end of the event.

Encouraging people who don't even have a roof over their heads to kiss bundles of banknotes before taking it from them feels cruel to me. But some of them are getting into the spirit, laughing and joking as they pose for pictures and film cameras.

Hornsleth tells me they come to him with ideas on how to make the project more controversial: "When we told our guys the name of the project was Hornsleth Homeless Tracker, they said 'no call it the Tramp Tracker, call it Hobo Tracker!' Once you give them a platform, they're full of ideas. When we show them our videos, we always think 'is this too much?' We're scared middle-class scum. They say 'you should have made it much more rough! Show it how it is, tell them the story.' Our videos are getting much more rough on our YouTube channel."

I wonder what sort of person would actually want to pay thousands of pounds to be able to track someone wherever they go. Frankly, it sounds downright creepy.

So when I speak to Jacob Risgaard, the Danish owner of online department store CoolShop.co.uk and one of the day's buyers, I'm surprised (and, in a way, relieved) when he tells me he's not actually interested in tracking anyone. For him it's about drawing attention to an issue he cares about.

He tells me: "We won't use [the tracker]. The tracking isn't that different to the way most apps track you on your phone, Facebook and Google know where you've been every minute. So if asked to hand over that data a year from now, I bet you 99% of the population would say yes – unless you have a secret lover somewhere.

"I'm really a bit boring, I know. The artist was a little bit angry with me about it but I wouldn't gain anything from [tracking someone] at all, personally.

"For me it's about trying to put focus on the homeless people, like now you're talking to me about this issue."

He adds that he also told Hornsleth to put the golden portrait of "his" homeless person up for auction to make more money for the participants.

I ask if it would not be better to simply give the money directly to the homeless people, rather than taking part in such a controversial stunt.

"You could say that," Risgaard admits, "and I agree. But if you look at the value of the publicity by being this controversial, they actually get much more than money out of it, they get focus on the situation they're in and I think for them it might be worth more than getting an extra meal."

While all those involved clearly seem to think what they're doing is a noble effort to raise awareness, homeless charity Centrepoint is less than convinced.

Paul Noblet, Centrepoint's Head of Public Affairs, say: "It is clearly a positive thing that a small number of people feel that they have been given a voice by the project, but the reality is that those who experience homelessness are not always heard and prioritised for government spending.

"Whilst this art project might highlight in the short term issues such as rough sleeping and sofa surfing, there is a danger that efforts to give a voice to the 150,000 young people who approach their local councils for help every year might be trivialised."

Hornsleth has no problem with admitting the project is exploitative.

"Of course it's slavery, we exploit them and they exploit us. And there's another word for that: business. It's not charity, it's business."

Has it ever gone too far?

"No, I think an art project can never go too far if you have the ethics with you, if you have the concrete idea. You can do anything you want if you can explain your story.

"My ethical code is getting rid of homelessness in Britain by any way we can do it."

I'm not entirely convinced, but ultimately I suppose I have to respect that everyone involved is happy.

As I leave, newly-purchased Bryan Gilchrist's message for critics of the project rings in my ears: "People give me money every day. This is a laugh. It's good fun and I'm not doing anything different than I would be doing if I wasn't taking part, except I've got a tracker. It only shows where I am, it doesn't show what I'm doing or who I'm with.

"Come and talk to us. Come and find us. I'm in Piccadilly all day, come and see me."

29 July 2017

⇨ The above information is reprinted with kind permission from The Huffington Post UK. Please visit www.huffingtonpost.co.uk for further information.

'Voice of the homeless' dies

Salutes to Jimmy Carlson, an inspirational activist and former solider, who was awarded an OBE for services to combatting homelessness, has died aged 69.

By Mark Lawrence

Jimmy was a former rough sleeper who spent nearly a quarter of a century living on the streets and in hostels – after five years serving as a soldier with the Royal Pioneer Corps.

Jimmy became abstinent from his alcohol addiction in 1996 and spent the next 20 years dedicating his life to tackling homelessness.

Jimmy began volunteering with the homelessness charity Groundswell in 1997 and was the leading figure at the organisation for 20 years – serving as a Trustee for the past five years. His passion was ensuring that homeless people themselves had a voice – and could be directly involved in tackling homelessness.

According to Groundswell Chief Executive, Athol Halle: "Homelessness has been on the rise for the past six years. Now more than ever we need inspirational leaders like Jimmy Carlson – to wake our society up to the fact that homelessness is unacceptable.

"Jimmy showed us that with passion and commitment you can achieve wonders – and that the best thing you can do for someone who is homeless is give them the opportunity to make a contribution."

Jimmy created the Homeless People's Commission with Groundswell – collecting homeless people's views from around the UK and presenting policy recommendations in the House of Lords in 2011.

Prior to that Jimmy delivered training on client involvement around the UK and was responsible for setting up numerous client involvement groups – including Outside In, the client involvement group for St Mungo's, London's largest homelessness service provider in 2006.

Jimmy was responsible for pioneering the 'Speakout' with Groundswell in the late 1990s' running hundreds of events around the country where homeless

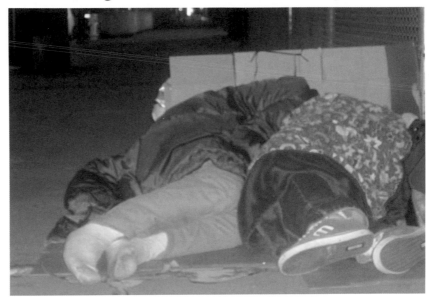

people could talk directly to those in power.

Jimmy also served as a Trustee for the Museum of Homelessness, and was preparing an exhibition to be launched at the Tate Modern in April 2017.

Jess Turtle, co-founder said: "Jimmy was instrumental in the development of the Museum of Homelessness; a champion, a wise counsel and a dear friend. This is a devastating loss for us and for the many others who knew and loved him."

Jimmy was also involved in setting up The Haven, a club where people in recovery from substance misuse could meet in an alcohol and drug-free environment, to help each other get their lives back on track. Starting with a £500 grant, Jimmy has raised over £100,000 to keep the club going.

Jimmy was born in Leeds in 1947 and passed away following respiratory health complications.

Jeremy Swain, the Chief Executive of leading homelessness charity Thames Reach, said: "For many years Jimmy Carlson had demons to battle which led to him becoming street homeless.

"Showing astonishing determination, Jimmy tackled his addiction problem and then went on to be a wonderful role model, working tirelessly to give people the confidence to take the

same journey as himself and holding the Government to account to tackle homelessness. We have lost a truly inspirational friend and colleague."

On receiving his OBE in the Queen's Birthday Honours in 2012, Jimmy Carlson said: "I am humbled to receive this honour. I have been to the very bottom and never would have imagined this day then. Lots of people have helped me on the way and I can only hope that my story can inspire others – the same way I have been helped."

"My message is never give up on anyone. You would have walked over me in the street 15 years ago and thought I was a lost cause, just another drunk. However, I picked myself up and turned my life around and I have gone on to make a decent contribution to my community.

"Rough sleepers you see on the street today – with the right support they have a lot to offer too. Never give up on anyone."

17 January 2017

⇨ The above information is reprinted with kind permission from 24housing. Please visit www.24housing.co.uk for further information.

It could happen to anyone – the banker's son who went from a £2 million home to homelessness

Ben Wardlaw enjoyed an upbringing of affluence and privilege. But he discovered that this cannot always defend young people against a life on the streets.

By Adam Lusher

He didn't grow up in one of London's £1 million homes. For Ben Wardlaw, it was more like £2 or £3 million, a five-bed Victorian terrace in west London. Father was a banker. Mother was a school governor.

Education meant private schools, including, briefly, Rugby, alma mater to MPs, baronets and viscounts, and to prime minister Neville Chamberlain.

He loved sailing. He was going to be a naval architect, "building and creating yachts". He certainly wasn't going to be homeless.

"The homeless," says Ben. "They weren't me. They were street sleepers, drug addicts, booze hounds. Aged 17, I deemed them human detritus, whom no one wanted to help or engage with."

But aged 17, just started in the upper sixth, he began to have serious problems with his mental health, the anger issues he was suffering causing serious tensions with his parents.

If now, at the age of 22, Ben can talk with authority about who the homeless really are, that's because all his privilege, all his education could do nothing to stop this banker's son becoming homeless himself.

Because in August 2013, when he was 19, the mental illness, the aggression that a loving family had been struggling to cope with, became too much.

Ben had a younger sister. One younger brother was 15, the other just nine.

"I was a threat," Ben explains, with no trace of rancour. "My parents had to make the choice between their ideals, and the safety of my sister and brothers. They said 'Look, we can't have you in the house'. It was awful. It sucked for everyone involved."

Ben the banker's son became Ben the sofa surfer, staying first with a grandmother, then a godmother. He slid further into mental illness.

"I was at rock bottom," he says. "You are supposed to come out of those public schools willing and able to take on the world. I felt robbed of that: absolutely isolated, unable to look towards the next day in a positive light, totally stagnant."

No wonder he is so exasperated – and amazed – at his 17-year-old self. "How could I ever have thought those things? How could I ever have been that arrogant, to think 'These aren't human beings; they are just what we don't want, but they stick around anyway'?"

At least now, there is an older, far wiser appreciation of all the forms that homelessness can take.

"They are the invisible homeless," he explains. "Four-fifths of them you will never, ever see. They are not rough sleeping, but in support accommodation, temporary accommodation, or sofa surfing. They have extraordinarily complex issues – mental health, physical health, family and emotional issues.

"These are people at the worst point in their lives."

And they often have no idea where to turn for help. Looking back at when he first started experiencing problems, Ben admits: "I didn't have a clue."

Nor did many of the other young homeless people that he later met: "The absolute vast majority of them didn't have a clue. Until someone decided to stick their neck out and help."

That, at least, is what happens to the lucky ones.

"The ones who aren't lucky," says Ben, "just disappear. I've had girls – and boys – telling me about having sex with someone to get a bed. They might resort to drugs or alcohol to take them away from the horrors they are facing. They can't deal with the fact that they can't sleep in a warm, sheltered place.

"They could die and no one would notice."

He was, he tells you, one of the lucky ones. Someone did decide to stick their neck out and help.

"My godmother drove me from Berkshire to London one Monday morning and I presented myself to mental health services round the back of Charing Cross Hospital in Fulham. They referred me to A and E to wait for the crisis psychiatric care team to assess me." It was a very long wait – almost too long.

"By the time I saw them, got them to write a letter to my local council explaining my condition, and then got to the council offices it was 4pm. The first thing the receptionist said to me was: 'Really? It's 4 o'clock. Did you really have to wait so long before turning up?'"

Many others, confidence destroyed, self-esteem battered, might have given up at the reception desk.

Ben persisted and had the good fortune to get to James, a council worker who was willing to stay after closing time to assess his needs.

By April 2014 he was in the care of Centrepoint, the charity for homeless young people. His experiences, he said, had taught him the need for the Young and Homeless helpline that Centrepoint is now trying to set up, with the help of *The Independent* and its Christmas charity appeal.

It might not solve the homelessness crisis on its own, says Ben, but such a helpline would mean fewer young people become the "unlucky ones", and many more find someone willing to stick their neck out.

"Just having someone there to back you," he says. "Someone in your corner, an advocate, to tell you 'I'm with you, we are going to get through this': you would be amazed at how important that is, just in terms of getting your confidence back.

"And what a helpline might do, is ensure that those people who do need help, get that help and aren't rebuffed by the receptionist who wants to go home."

He adds, after some thought: "I would say it would save lives. [Some studies have shown], if you are homeless, you are ten times more likely to die earlier. So there is a very real proportion of those young people who aren't being helped who will, sadly, die prematurely. With a helpline, that will, hopefully, decrease."

During his seven-month stay at Centrepoint's west London facility, Ben decided "to become a bit of a yes man, to soak up everything they had to offer".

They had a lot to offer. It "snowballed" from psychotherapy, to standing for election and becoming chairman of Centrepoint Parliament, which gives a voice to young homeless people. He played tennis with Tim Henman when he announced a partnership with Centrepoint; he attended the Downton Abbey fundraising ball.

"Hope returns. You are doing all this amazing stuff. You realise that there is a life to look forward to."

Ben is living independently now, in a studio flat. His relationship with his parents is "trending in the right direction." He has worked for PR firms, is in the process of launching his own business, and is a sergeant instructor in the Army Cadet Force.

The desire to design yachts for the wealthy may have gone. But it seems

to have been replaced by something else: a new passion for speaking out on behalf of the people he once disdained, but later joined.

As he prepares say goodbye, he is determined to stress just one more thing, something that five years ago a 17-year-old boy in a multimillion pound house would have scoffed at.

"It's really important," he urges, "that homeless people aren't written off."

Then comes the wry acknowledgement: "Centrepoint put me back on track. Yes, it was a different track to the one before, but I'm so much happier on this railway."

22 November 2016

⇨ The above information is reprinted with kind permission from *The Independent*. Please visit www.independent.co.uk for further information.

© independent.co.uk 2018

Homelessness charity launches free sanitary products initiative

Simon Community Scotland is launching a Period Friendly Point service to provide sanitary products to homeless women in Glasgow and Edinburgh.

By Georgina Harris

Homelessness charity Simon Community Scotland is supporting homeless women by offering free sanitary products in Glasgow and Edinburgh.

The charity provides practical support to people who are homeless, as well as working to tackle the causes of homelessness. Its street team provides first aid and basics such as food, needle exchange and sleeping bags.

Simon Community Scotland will provide packs designed to last for 48 hours containing sanitary products, spare underwear, wipes and disposable bags, plus small information booklets about wider services that may be useful to these women, such as healthcare and housing.

The packs are being called Period Friendly Pax and they will be available and regularly replenished at various points throughout Glasgow and Edinburgh.

Trained staff will be handing out the packs at Period Friendly Points to speak to women about issues such as personal health and hygiene.

A recent survey by Simon Community Scotland found that 70% of women using its supported accommodation services had never been told what a period is, nor spoken to anyone about their period. 61% also said they used toilet paper or newspaper during their period because they couldn't afford sanitary products.

The charity is launching with three Period Friendly Points in Glasgow and two in Edinburgh, and hopes to extend the service to other Scottish towns and cities in the future.

Last week, Scottish Labour MSP Monica Lennon started a consultation process at the Scottish Parliament to make it a legal right to be able to access sanitary products, including a duty on schools, colleges and universities across Scotland to provide them for free in female toilets.

Lorraine McGrath, chief executive at Simon Community Scotland, said: "Homeless women often didn't have the opportunity to discuss their periods with their mother, at school or with peers as a consequence of

23

traumatic childhood and institutional care.

"The women are often embarrassed to talk about their periods or ask for sanitary products when they need them and have no means to purchase them.

"For women on the street, and even in supported services, they will often choose to buy food, alcohol, drugs or a bed for the night rather than sanitary products."

Monica Lennon also commented: "This is an inspiring initiative from Simon Community Scotland.

"Access to sanitary products is about maintaining basic human rights and dignity.

"I'm glad that the Simon Community are taking this initiative forward. It's also why I've launched a consultation on a members' bill proposal in the Scottish Parliament to ensure that there is free access to sanitary products for anyone who needs them – you can find out more and give your responses on the consultation by visiting our Period Poverty website."

McGrath added: "Being homeless is bad enough – poor accommodation, lack of sleep and poor nutrition, with only the clothes you stand in.

"Period Friendly Points will ensure women on the streets do not go without sanitary products and have access to the support they need."

23 August 2017

⇨ The above information is reprinted with kind permission from Third Force News. Please visit www.thirdforcenews.org.uk for further information.

Young people's experiences of hidden homelessness

An extract from Danger zones and stepping stones.

By Sarah McCoy and Becky Hug

Do young people use the term 'sofa surfing'? What do they understand it to mean? And do they think it is useful?

Not a term used by young people: "I've heard it with professionals, but that's about it."

Before the introduction of the term by researchers, six of the 14 interviewees whose comments were analysed for this section had mentioned 'sofa surfing' spontaneously during their interview to describe their experiences. When prompted, only one young person said they had not come across the term before.

While this suggests that awareness of the term is high among young people, and that some would describe their experiences as 'sofa surfing', it does not tell us whether they are using the term because they feel it is an appropriate description of their experiences or because of external influences. After further investigation, evidence was gathered to suggest that 'sofa surfing' is a term used more by practitioners, academics and the media than by young people themselves.

The young people we spoke to told us the term was used by "older people" and professionals rather than by their peers, and they had heard it used on television.

"My parents, they would say 'Are you going out sofa surfing?' if I was to stay out during the week."

(Grace, 19, South East)

"I've never heard it, well I've heard it with professionals but that's about it."

(Jon, 18, North West)

"None of my mates use [the term] but, when I normally watch TV about the homeless and all that stuff… I actually hear it a lot on there."

(Reece, 17, North West)

The majority of the young people involved in the research said they had first heard the term used by professionals, usually when they had engaged with some sort of support service. Several recounted experiences of services categorising their experiences as 'sofa surfing' either when they presented themselves at a service or while receiving support. For instance, one young person said they first heard the term when they were given a support worker:

"I remember her saying, 'you don't want to be sofa surfing like the rest of them'."

(Amelia, 16, North East)

Risks can be underestimated: "It makes light of a serious situation"

Sofa surfing is an umbrella term that encompasses a wide range of living arrangements – both safe and very dangerous. In general, while young people could see the merits of having a term to describe a set of experiences that it would be difficult to categorise otherwise, they felt the term had a number of disadvantages.

Some felt that use of the term could lead to the risks being underestimated. This may be as a consequence of confusion regarding what the term means, or because of the actual phrase, which can sometimes appear light-hearted.

"I don't think it's a very good term because [sofa surfing] doesn't always mean you have a sofa to sleep on… you could be on the floor or in someone's cupboard but you say to people 'sofa surfing', they just assume that you've got a sofa to sleep on but sometimes that's not the case…"

(Matthew, 22, South East)

"It sounds funny and makes light of a situation that is serious."

(Emma, 19, North East)

How do young people fall out of secure accommodation?

All the young people we spoke to had experience of falling out of stable accommodation and into more transient and temporary living arrangements. The reasons for these transitions were varied, but some common themes emerged.

Relationship breakdown: "I got kicked out of my mum's."

The young people involved in this research were most likely to have found themselves in temporary living situations because of a breakdown in family relationships. Nearly half of the interviewees said tensions in their family home were the primary reason they lost stable accommodation. For one young person, it was their foster placement that broke down rather than relations with their birth family.

Personality clashes were frequently mentioned, as were issues such as drug use that caused conflict between young people and their parents.

"Basically the reason why [Mum] kicked me out was because I was going through stopping smoking cannabis and I was going through stopping smoking as well.

So obviously I had mood swings and [my mother's partner] couldn't put up with me."

(Christopher, 21, South East)

While some young people were asked to leave their family home, others chose to do so to avoid the stress of family life.

For more than one young person, the decision to leave was influenced by fear for their personal safety as they were subjected to domestic abuse.

"Because [my Dad] was going out with this girl… and she kept beating me up for certain things that I'd do, like if I had a fag, she'd beat me up, or took something that weren't mine, she'd beat me up."

(Reece, 17, North West)

There was evidence that more subtle forms of abuse may have also influenced young people's decisions to leave their family home. For example, one young person cited excessively controlling parents and a lack of personal privacy as the main reason he fell out of stable accommodation:

"If I was there, I wasn't allowed to go to my room, I had to sit in the living room all day… there'd be no conversation in the room whatsoever… I wasn't allowed to have my bedroom door shut at night, just stupid little things that made me really unhappy. That's why I had to leave."

(Matthew, 22, South East)

Which different types of temporary accommodation are young people experiencing?

Staying with friends

Almost all the young people who were interviewed said they had stayed with friends at some point when they were without stable accommodation. However, with the rise of Facebook and other forms of social media, the concept of 'friends' has become increasingly ill defined, particularly among young people. In line with this, the young people we spoke to used the phrase 'staying with friends' when describing a wide range of experiences.

Some young people stayed with very close friends, often those they had known throughout their childhood. If these situations occurred at a young age, this usually meant the young people stayed in the family homes of their friends where they were supported by their friends' parents and, in some cases, "treated as one of the family". These were often very positive experiences, where young people were made to feel welcome and comfortable.

"Yeah, she's basically my mum, that's what I class her as, I call her 'mum' and stuff like that because I've known him [the friend] like 11 years, so it's just family basically, that's what I class it as."

(Sean, 18, North East)

Staying with family

It is often assumed that staying with family members is low risk in the context of temporary living. However, the young people we spoke to described a variety of experiences within this category. Several were far from positive, and some pushed them further into instability and homelessness.

One young man reported being "in good shape and good health" before moving to another city to stay temporarily with his uncle. It soon became apparent that his uncle was a heavy user of drugs and alcohol, and as a result of this influence, the young man started using hard drugs himself. His mental health suffered and his living arrangements broke down, leading to a six-week period of rough sleeping.

"[Staying with my uncle] was quite difficult. He had a dealer living in the house and it wasn't like cannabis, it was hard-core drugs… I had a complete mental breakdown after that like and I kicked off, I was homeless."

(Josh, 23, North East)

Large hostels and refuges

From our sample, there were no examples of positive experiences of larger hostels recounted. Instead, young people spoke of being exposed to negative influences, such as drugs and alcohol, and of a lack of adequate support. There were some graphic descriptions of what it was like to live in these hostels, which sounded far from suitable for young people.

"I couldn't even walk out my room without shoes or socks on because there could be needles or something all over the hostel."

(Jon, 18, North West)

"It's just like a massive hostel but it's got, like, the people there were more rough, they're a lot older... most people that are in there are like ex-druggies, alcoholics and stuff like that."

(Carly, 19, Yorkshire and the Humber)

B&Bs and other councilcommissioned short-term accommodation

Relatively few of the young people interviewed had experience of staying in B&Bs or other short-term accommodation commissioned by their local authorities.

This may reflect recent efforts within the housing sector to avoid placing young people in such accommodation in response to evidence to suggest that it is unsuitable for their needs. (House of Commons Education Select Committee 2014).

While the evidence base paints a largely negative picture of B&Bs as a form of temporary accommodation for young people, opinions among those interviewed were mixed, with some young people speaking positively about their experiences and others less so.

While one young person described a B&B he had stayed in as "the best place I ever, ever lived in my whole life", it should be noted that this was largely because he got on so well with the people around him when he had previously been subjected to bullying and abuse. There were no examples of such experiences helping young people to progress in their lives or take steps towards stable accommodation.

Smaller accommodation services for young people

Depaul provides supported accommodation that is exclusively for young people in projects that typically house no more than 20 residents at any one time. Although young people are able to stay in projects like Depaul's for a considerable amount of time (up to around two years), we have included them as a type of temporary living arrangement in the context of this report because the accommodation provided is not permanent. Instead, the intention is to work with young people while they are living in the projects to prepare them for independent living.

All but two of the young people we spoke to were living in small Depaul accommodation projects at the time of their interview. It is possible that young people's comments were influenced to some degree by the fact they were speaking to Depaul staff. However, attitudes towards the type of accommodation Depaul provides was resoundingly positive.

Despite the transient nature of their stay, the young people we spoke to felt more secure in Depaul accommodation than they had at other stages of their temporary living journeys. This was partially because the projects they were staying in were for the exclusive use of young people, and either staffed on a 24-hour basis or strictly supervised. This, for the large part, protects young people from exposure to the negative influences that are so widespread in larger establishments. The young people we spoke to described the atmosphere in their projects as generally "calm" and "easy going".

This sense of security also appeared to be related to the fact the majority of the young people spoke highly of, and had built strong relationships with, project staff. One young person described how he felt both physically and emotionally secure in his project as a result of having staff around that he could be open and honest with:

"It helps just them being there, just knowing that if I hear a noise downstairs, it's nothing to worry about. And I know that I can come down here and talk to [the staff] about absolutely anything. They're not going to judge me, just give me their honest opinions, which is a big comfort."

(Matthew, 22, South East)

Nightstop

Three of the young people we spoke to had experience of using Depaul's volunteer-based service, Nightstop, in which young people are provided with a place to stay in the home of vetted volunteers.

They all considered Nightstop useful respite and found it considerably better than "being cold on the streets", which tallies with previous research

by Insley (2011) in which 15 out of 18 respondents said they felt safer at Nightstop than in their previous living situation.

One of the young people had been housed in the home of a fairly affluent family and had felt "awkward" in "posh" surroundings.

Because of this, and the influence of a friend who advised him against staying with "randomers", this young person only used the service once.

"It was a bit awkward, they were really posh, like she sat there and played the piano in the living room and... it was like really high standard flats in the city centre. It's too high up for me in a way."

(Sean, 18, North East)

Rough sleeping – the alternative to temporary living arrangements

'Rough sleeping' is not accommodation, so we would not consider it to be a temporary living arrangement comparable to those we have described above. We have included it here, however, as it is important to acknowledge the types of scenario young people are trying to avoid by entering into the temporary arrangements we have described.

'Rough sleeping' featured prominently in the experiences of the young people involved in the research. Most had experience of 'rough sleeping' between temporary living arrangements, usually falling to such options when they had exhausted all other alternatives. However, it is important to note that 'rough sleeping' is yet another term that is difficult to define, highly complex and denotes a diverse range of situations.

The young people used terms such as 'sleeping rough', 'sleeping on the streets' and 'properly homeless' to describe a variety of experiences, including but not limited to:

⇨ Sleeping in squats with existing friends or strangers

⇨ Sleeping on all-night buses or trains

⇨ Spending the night in 24-hour restaurants or cafés

- Staying with other homeless people in large homeless "camps"
- Breaking into and sleeping in cars
- Sleeping on the streets.

While none of these options are safe, the level and type of risk presented varies. It is important, therefore, that when a young person describes themselves as sleeping rough, their specific circumstances are explored to understand accurately the risks to which they are exposed.

Interestingly, while 'rough sleeping' was considered by the majority of the young people to be the least appealing of all temporary living options, one interviewee was very clear that he would prefer to sleep rough than in the home of a stranger because he would feel safer outside with CCTV than in someone's home where "anything could happen". Another said they would rather sleep outdoors than in the house of a volunteer because he would feel like he was being judged for being homeless, highlighting the importance of ensuring that crisis accommodation for young people is non-judgemental and appropriate for their needs

"I'd sleep on streets before I'd sleep at someone's I don't know. The housing agency offered me [a room] with someone for three days or something, like three days a week and move to different people's houses, but I was having none of it, I said to them I'd rather be on streets."

(Simon, 19, North West)

21 March 2016

- The above information is reprinted with kind permission from Depaul UK. Please visit www.uk.depaulcharity.org for further information.

© 2018 Depaul UK

Britain's dark history of criminalising homeless people in public spaces

*An article from **The Conversation**.*

By Victoria Cooper, Lecturer in Social Policy and Criminology, The Open University and Daniel McCulloch, Lecturer in Criminology and Social Policy, The Open University

Since the onset of austerity in 2010, the estimated number of people sleeping rough in England has more than doubled, from 1,768 in 2010, to 4,134 in 2016. As the number of homeless people increases, while support services and hostels are diminishing, rough sleepers are becoming ever more visible in British cities.

But rather than finding ways to accommodate the homeless, the UK Government has sought to criminalise them. From archaic vagrancy laws, to the more recent Public Spaces Protection Orders (PSPOs), governments have been passing new laws and reviving old ones which result in the punishment of people with no fixed abode.

People without access to land or property are denied the freedom to roam, sit, eat, wash or sleep in public spaces. Or, where local authorities do lawfully permit street homeless people to access and use public spaces (for homeless camps, homeless shelters or day centres), these sites are routinely monitored by criminal justice agencies, bringing the homeless under direct surveillance and control.

Modern day vagrants

The criminalisation of the homeless can be traced back to 1824 and beyond, when vagrancy laws were implemented to control the spread of 'urban poverty' at the height of the Industrial Revolution. During this time, land privatisation was being rolled out on a mass scale, and hundreds of thousands of people who lacked the means to purchase property were displaced from their homes and prohibited from accessing the land they once lived on.

Vagrancy laws criminalised access to land in cases where there was no contractual relationship, which gave police the power to arrest people who were not legally bound to property or land. These individuals were characterised as 'incorrigible rogues' and 'mobile anomalies' by the law, and punished with flogging, incarceration and even transportation to penal colonies such as Australia.

Fast forward almost two centuries, and these antiquated laws – and imperious attitudes – are still very much with us. In the period from 2006 to 2014, the number of court cases for 'vagrancy-related offences' in England increased by 70% – from 1,510 prosecutions to 2,365. The most noteworthy cases involved three men who were very nearly prosecuted for taking food waste from a supermarket refuse bin, and an operation in Sussex involving undercover police, which led to the arrest of 60 rough sleepers for accepting money from the public.

Hostile streets

This is the work of successive governments. Civil orders introduced under Tony Blair to target 'street-crime' effectively led to a clampdown on begging, which sanctioned homeless communities en masse. When the Coalition Government came to power in 2010, these civil orders were amended to give local authorities even greater powers over what people do in public spaces.

In particular, Public Spaces Protection Orders (PSPOs), brought in under the 2014 Anti-social Behaviour, Crime and Policing Act, allowed local authorities to enforce on-the-spot fines for certain activities. Predictably, local authorities are applying these new powers to target homeless people by sanctioning what they do in public spaces: street drinking, begging, camping in parks, defecating and urinating and in some cases even sleeping.

Not only do PSPOs criminalise the homeless, they also make these tactics appear as a local response to a perceived problem and avoids the exposure and opposition which national measures usually invoke. Yet PSPOs are not a local response: their use is widespread across England,

and it's increasing, with one in ten local authorities now using PSPOs to criminalise homeless people.

To make matters worse, private owners of commercial land are boarding-up shop doorways, erecting spikes and using possession laws to forcibly remove the homeless from commercial spaces.

The fight for the right to exist

Yet there have been moments of resistance against these anti-homeless measures. Both campaigns by organisations such as Liberty, and individuals like the family who placed cushions over anti-homeless spikes in Manchester, are challenging the punitive measures adopted by local authorities. In some areas this has led to the successful withdrawal of PSPO proposals.

In austerity Britain, these movements are gathering momentum and stirring up indignation about the uneven distribution of wealth, property and land. Some resistance movements are even occupying empty properties to make space for homeless people and

homeless communities themselves are documenting their own daily struggle as they fight for the right to exist in public spaces.

Homelessness itself is not yet a crime, but anti-homeless laws and strategies are restricting homeless people's freedom, and turning everyday activities into punishable offences. Yet survival defines the daily lives of homeless people, and in the face of oppression they will find new ways to expose the violence and prejudice they encounter in the every day.

10 March 2017

⇨ The above information is reprinted with kind permission from *The Conversation*. Please visit www.theconversation.com for further information.

© 2010-2018, The Conversation Trust (UK)

How politicians can prevent more homeless people from dying on the streets

***An article from* The Conversation.**

THE CONVERSATION

By Graham Bowpitt, Reader in Social Policy, Nottingham Trent University

Politicians reacted with shock and sadness to the news that a homeless man was found dead on 14 February at Westminster tube station, by the back entrance to the Houses of Parliament.

It has been reported that the man, who was Portuguese, had been staying in one homeless shelter, but had outstayed the maximum time allowed there. So he was sleeping rough while waiting for another space in a shelter elsewhere.

The graphic, first-hand encounter with the actuality of homelessness has prompted calls from politicians for tough action to tackle rough sleeping. Little has been revealed of the immediate circumstances of this man's death, but he is not the only homeless person to die on the streets. A study for the homelessness charity Crisis found that 1,731 homeless people died in England between 2001 and 2009.

In 2017, there was a 15% rise in the number of people sleeping rough in the UK – and Westminster was no exception. In autumn 2017, Westminster was the local authority with the highest number of rough sleepers in England – 217 people.

Complex lives on the margins

Politicians calling for further action should reflect on the failure of recent policies to prevent rough sleeping. For instance, short-term prisoners are still discharged to 'no fixed abode' despite the 2014 Offender Rehabilitation Act, which set up Community Rehabilitation Companies to support all prisoners on discharge, including help to secure accommodation.

My recent research in Nottingham revealed that persistent rough sleepers still face a complex set of needs. Rough sleepers who spent at least 10% of their nights on the streets in 2016–17, or who slept rough for part of the time during at least three out of the last six years, were more likely than other homeless people to need support for problematic substance use, mental ill health and offending. They were also more likely to have spent significant time in prison, and to have been evicted from accommodation or excluded from or refused services.

People disabled by negative experiences find themselves ill-equipped to negotiate what they encounter as an increasingly hostile system. That system currently offers a limited range of options in available hostels or affordable private rented accommodation. Even access to these options can be further thwarted by restrictions faced by homeless migrants on welfare benefits, or by accumulated debts or the strictures of a benefit system that might make begging appear a more rewarding source of income.

The very homelessness legislation that was set up to respond to the needs of homeless people merely erects further barriers to rough sleepers. It fails to recognise them as 'vulnerable' and denies them a connection to the local authority to which they are applying for assistance – even when they may be fleeing violence. Some people are also declared 'intentionally homeless' if they refuse offers of accommodation out of fear.

Carrying baggage

People often ask why some rough sleepers reject help when it is offered, and the popular conclusion that is often drawn – even by some politicians – is that persistent rough sleepers are sleeping rough out of choice.

But sleeping on the streets is rarely the only problem that persistent rough sleepers have. Often they have a complex set of needs and experiences of domestic violence and personal victimisation. Many of them carry a baggage of negative risk assessments by people such as hostel staff that might have arisen from past anti social behaviour, accumulated indebtedness, eviction, rejection, disqualification and disentitlement. Such assessments are recorded and shared among agencies locally, thereby barring people from whatever accommodation and other services that might be on offer.

Meanwhile, those without such a reputation often refuse offers of accommodation out of fear of who they might encounter, either in a hostel or in a particular neighbourhood where they would be housed. Or they may abandon such offers when their fears are justified by experiences of violence, exploitation or intimidation. They may also attach greater importance to a valued relationship with a partner or friend than to an offer of accommodation in which that person cannot be included.

In April, the new Homelessness Reduction Act 2017 will come into force. It brings new obligations on local authorities to prevent and relieve the situations of all homeless people, not just those in priority need and with a local connection. The Government says it wants to eliminate rough sleeping by 2027. If politicians want to be true to their word, they must ensure local authorities have the resources to respond effectively to those who find themselves with no alternative to a life on the streets.

19 February 2018

⇨ The above information is reprinted with kind permission from *The Conversation*. Please visit www.theconversation.com for further information.

Strangers are working together to crowdfund people out of homelessness

"Drink and drugs had completely ruined my life."

By Natasha Hinde

This time last year Joe was living in a hostel. He'd become homeless following a relationship break-up and spent the following 14 months moving between temporary accommodation.

The Londoner was desperately trying to get his life back on track, having kicked a 20-year drink and drug addiction which had "completely ruined" his life. He had tried various avenues to find work, but was finding it almost impossible to secure employment.

Fast forward to today and the 37-year-old has turned his life around thanks to the kindness of strangers and an app called Beam, which crowdfunds to help homeless people train and get into work.

Joe now lives in a one bedroom flat and has a full-time job working as a slinger signaller, assisting with crane operations on a building site. "I'm in a very happy place," he says. "It's great that people out there would do that, just give money to someone like myself. They should be proud of themselves."

His story is a lesson in sheer willpower and defiance. "All the guys in the hostel were still drinking and using drugs, so it was a horrible place to be in. But I was so determined to get a job," he recalls. "Drink and drugs had completely ruined my life, so the more it was getting thrown in my face, the more I was determined to move forward."

Joe tried relentlessly to find himself work. He pursued a loan, and then attempted to obtain funding from the Job Centre to get trained, but it wasn't to be. "I was getting knocked down at every corner," he says. "Everywhere I tried it just wasn't happening. Then I got introduced to Beam through one of the women working at Thames Reach hostel and it all changed."

Beam is the world's first crowdfunding platform of its kind. Backed by the Mayor of London, the app launched in September and has since funded 22 campaigns, raising over £67,000 from public donations to fund a range of industry-recognised qualifications.

There are over 1,200 supporters and 23 homeless members on the platform who are pursuing a range of career paths – from electricians and accountants to teaching assistants and social workers.

Claudia Green, 28, is one of Beam's first supporters. She donated £20 to Joe's campaign, which reached £1,132 in five days, and has followed his progress throughout.

"Seeing Joe's progress has been amazing and satisfying, everything seemed to happen pretty quickly," she says. "When I first saw the campaign my reaction was: Ok this is going to take a while to get him from homeless status to full-time employment. But it felt like, within weeks, I'd been updated that he had his work gear, had passed his certification and was ready to apply for a job."

While a lot of people don't see where their money goes when they give to charity, the beauty of Beam is that it sends updates to contributors throughout – so they can really see the difference they've made. "We need more charities like this," says Claudia. "Beam gives them all the tools to change their circumstances."

Statistics from charity Shelter suggest there are more than 307,000 homeless people in Britain. Alex Stephany, Beam's founder and CEO, says his app is creating a "long-term solution to homelessness that everyone can be a part of".

"I met Joe when we were launching Beam just over six months ago," Alex recalls, adding that Joe's success story shows that the app could change the fate of thousands more.

Recalling the moment he received donations on Beam, Joe says: "It made me feel so much happier and put more determination into what I wanted to do. It was uplifting, that's for sure – because it's just strangers giving to you for no reason really. It's just out of pure kindness."

He finished his training in October 2017 and it then took three months to find work. "It didn't get me down or nothing," he says. "I knew I was going to get a job somewhere. And then I did."

He is now a slinger signaller working for VGC Group using tower and crawler cranes on the Northern Line extension at Battersea. "It's a wicked job, with really nice people working alongside me, it's really good," he adds.

When asked if he has a message for the people who helped him, he gushes:

"They really, really have helped me. It might've seemed nothing to them that they were giving money... but it's changed my life, that's for sure."

9 April 2018

⇨ The above information is reprinted with kind permission from The Huffington Post UK. Please visit www.huffingtonpost.co.uk for further information.

© 2018 Oath (UK) Limited

New grant for council homelessness services

The flexible homelessness support grant will give councils greater flexibility to prioritise homelessness prevention.

From Ministry of Housing, Communities and Local Government and Marcus Jones, MP

The Government is transforming the way councils fund homelessness services, giving them greater flexibility to prioritise homelessness prevention, Communities Minister Marcus Jones has confirmed.

The new 'flexible homelessness support grant' is a radical replacement of the tightly controlled funding currently given to source and manage temporary accommodation for homeless individuals and their families.

Under the existing 'temporary accommodation management fee', funding can only be used for expensive intervention when a household is already homeless, rather than on preventing this happening in the first place.

The new grant will empower councils with the freedom to support the full range of homelessness services. This could include employing a homelessness prevention or tenancy support officer to work closely with people who are at risk of losing their homes.

Communities Minister Marcus Jones said:

"This Government is determined to help the most vulnerable in society, which is why we're investing £550 million to 2020 to tackle homelessness and rough sleeping.

"We've brought in a raft of measures over the last few months, from funding homelessness projects in 225 local authorities to changing the law by backing Bob Blackman's Homelessness Reduction Bill to support for more people at risk of losing their homes.

"We're now going further and giving councils greater flexibility, so they can move away from costly intervention when a household is already homeless, to preventing this happening in the first place."

Councils across England will receive £402 million over the next two years. No local authority will receive less annual funding under the grant than we estimate they would have received under the Department for Work and Pensions fee. First-year allocations will also include an additional amount

to authorities with high temporary accommodation commitments.

Compared to the old system, we estimate that London councils will receive around £20 million more next year and that other high-pressure areas, including Leeds, Birmingham, Reading, Peterborough and Portsmouth, will also gain significant additional funding.

In recognition of the particular pressures which London councils face, we are also setting aside £25 million of the funding across the two years while we work with the Greater London Authority and London boroughs to look at how we might help councils collaborate in the procurement of accommodation for homeless families in London.

The new grant forms part of the wide range of measures the Government is taking to prevent people from becoming homeless.

This includes:

⇨ protecting and maintaining the funding for councils to provide homelessness prevention services at £315 million over the four years to 2019–20; £20 million to support innovative approaches in local areas to tackle and prevent homelessness

⇨ a £20-million rough sleeping prevention fund to help individuals at risk or new to the streets get back on their feet

⇨ a £10-million Social Impact Bond programme to help long-term rough sleepers

⇨ £61 million for councils to implement the measures in the Homelessness Reduction Bill, which will change the law to provide vital support for more people at risk of losing their homes.

Further information

The former Chancellor announced at Autumn Statement 2015 that the Department for Work and Pensions' temporary accommodation management fee would be replaced by a Department for Communities and Local Government grant from April 2017.

The new flexible homelessness support grant will come in from 1 April 2017. It is based on a completely new funding model so resources are directed to the areas with the greatest need and which allows councils to plan their homelessness services with certainty.

The funding allocated for the two years from 2017 to 2018 is £186 million and £191 million. A further £25 million has been set aside for London boroughs to work together to provide accommodation for homeless families in the capital.

15 March 2017

⇨ The above information is reprinted with kind permission from Gov. uk. Please visit www.gov.uk for further information.

Overview of the homelessness legislation

A summary of the homelessness legislation and the duties, powers and obligations on housing authorities and others towards people who are homeless or threatened with homelessness.

1. This overview provides a summary of the homelessness legislation and the duties, powers and obligations on housing authorities and others towards people who are homeless or at risk of homelessness. It does not form part of the statutory code of guidance.

The homelessness legislation

2. The primary homelessness legislation – that is, Part 7 of the Housing Act 1996 – provides the statutory under-pinning for action to prevent homelessness and provide assistance to people threatened with or who are actually homeless.

3. In 2002, the Government amended the homelessness legislation through the Homelessness Act 2002 and the Homelessness (Priority Need for Accommodation) (England) Order 2002 to:

   (a) ensure a more strategic approach to tackling and preventing homelessness, in particular by requiring a homelessness strategy for every housing authority district; and

   (b) strengthen the assistance available to people who are homeless or threatened with homelessness by extending the priority need categories to homeless 16- and 17-year-olds; care leavers aged 18, 19 and 20; people who are vulnerable as a result of time spent in care, the armed forces, prison or custody, and people who are vulnerable because they have fled their home because of violence.

4. The Homelessness Reduction Act 2017 significantly reformed England's homelessness legislation by placing duties on local authorities to intervene at earlier stages to prevent homelessness in their areas. It also requires housing authorities to provide homelessness services to all those affected, not just those who have 'priority need'. These include:

   (a) an enhanced prevention duty extending the period a household is threatened with homelessness from 28 days to 56 days, meaning that housing authorities are required to work with people to prevent homelessness at an earlier stage; and

   (b) a new duty for those who are already homeless so that housing authorities will support households for 56 days to relieve their homelessness by helping them to secure accommodation.

Homelessness review and strategy

5. Under the Homelessness Act 2002, all housing authorities must have in place a homelessness strategy based on a review of all forms of homelessness in their district. The strategy must be renewed at least every five years. The social services authority must provide reasonable assistance.

6. The strategy must set out the authority's plans for the prevention of homelessness and for securing that sufficient accommodation and support are or will be available for people who become homeless or who are at risk of becoming so.

Duty to refer

7. The Homelessness Reduction Act 2017 introduced a duty on certain public authorities to refer service users who they think may be homeless or threatened with homelessness to a housing authority. The service user must give consent, and can choose which authority to be referred to. The housing authority should incorporate the duty to refer into their homelessness strategy and establish effective partnerships and working arrangements with agencies to facilitate appropriate referrals.

Duty to provide advisory services

8. The housing authority has a duty to provide advice and information about homelessness and the prevention of homelessness and the rights of homeless people or those at risk of homelessness, as well as the help that is available from the housing authority or others and how to access that help. The service should be designed with certain listed vulnerable groups in mind and authorities can provide it themselves or arrange for other agencies to do it on their behalf.

Applications and inquiries

9. Housing authorities must give proper consideration to all applications for housing assistance, and if they have reason to believe that an applicant may be homeless or threatened with homelessness, they must make inquiries to see whether they owe them any duty under Part 7 of the 1996 Act. This assessment process is important in enabling housing authorities to identify the assistance which an applicant may need, either to prevent them from becoming homeless, or to help them to find another home. In each case, the authority will need to first decide whether the applicant is eligible for assistance and threatened with or actually homeless. Certain applicants who are 'persons from abroad' are not eligible for any assistance under Part 7 except free advice and information about homelessness and the prevention of homelessness.

10. Broadly speaking, a person is threatened with homelessness if they are likely to become homeless within 56 days. An applicant who has been served with valid notice under section 21 of the Housing Act 1988 to end their assured shorthold tenancy is also threatened with homelessness, if the notice has expired or will expire within 56 days and is served in respect of the only accommodation that is available for them to occupy.

11. An applicant is to be considered homeless if they do not have accommodation that they have a legal right to occupy, which is accessible and physically available to them (and their household) and which it would be reasonable for them to continue to live in.

Assessments and personalised housing plans

12. Housing authorities have a duty to carry out an assessment in all cases where an eligible applicant is homeless or threatened with homelessness. This will identify what has caused the homelessness or threat of homelessness, the housing needs of the applicant and any support they need in order to be able to secure and retain accommodation. Following this assessment, the housing authority must work with the person to develop a personalised housing plan which will include actions (or 'reasonable steps') to be taken by the authority and the applicant to try and prevent or relieve homelessness.

Prevention duty

13. Housing authorities have a duty to take reasonable steps to help prevent any eligible person (regardless of priority need status, intentionality and whether they have a local connection) who is threatened with homelessness from becoming homeless. This means either helping them to stay in their current accommodation or helping them to find a new place to live before they become actually homeless. The prevention duty continues for 56 days unless it is brought to an end by an event such as accommodation being secured for the person, or by their becoming homeless.

Relief duty

14. If the applicant is already homeless, or becomes homeless despite activity during the prevention stage, the reasonable steps will be focused on helping the applicant to secure accommodation. This relief duty lasts for 56 days unless ended in another way. If the housing authority has reason to believe a homeless applicant may be eligible for assistance and have a priority need they must be provided with interim accommodation.

Main housing duty

15. If homelessness is not successfully prevented or relieved, a housing authority will owe the main housing duty to applicants who are eligible, have a priority need for accommodation and are not homeless intentionally. Certain categories of household, such as pregnant women, families with children, and households that are homeless due to an emergency such as a fire or flood, have priority need if homeless. Other groups may be assessed as having priority need because they are vulnerable as a result of old age, mental ill health, physical disability, having been in prison or care or as a result of becoming homeless due to domestic abuse.

16. Under the main housing duty, housing authorities must ensure that suitable accommodation is available for the applicant and

their household until the duty is brought to an end, usually through the offer of a settled home. The duty can also be brought to an end for other reasons, such as the applicant turning down a suitable offer of temporary accommodation or because they are no longer eligible for assistance. A suitable offer of a settled home (whether accepted or refused by the applicant) which would bring the main housing duty to an end includes an offer of a suitable secure or introductory tenancy with a local authority, an offer of accommodation through a private registered provider (also known as a housing association) or the offer of a suitable tenancy for at least 12 months from a private landlord made by arrangement with the local authority.

Suitable accommodation

17. Housing authorities have various powers and duties to secure accommodation for homeless applicants, either on an interim basis, to prevent or relieve homelessness, to meet the main housing duty or as a settled home. Accommodation must always be 'suitable' and there are particular standards set when private rented accommodation is secured for households which have priority need.

18. Under the Homelessness (Suitability of Accommodation) (England) Order 2003, bed and breakfast accommodation is not considered suitable for families with children and households that include a pregnant woman, except where there is no other accommodation available, and then only for a maximum of six weeks. The Secretary of State considers that bed and breakfast accommodation is unsuitable for 16- and 17-year-olds.

Intentional homelessness

19. A person would be homeless intentionally where homelessness was the consequence of a deliberate action or omission by that person. A deliberate act might be a decision to leave the previous accommodation even though it would have been reasonable for the person (and everyone in the person's household) to continue to live there. A deliberate omission might be non-payment of rent that led to rent arrears and eviction despite the rent being affordable.

20. Where people have a priority need but are intentionally homeless the housing authority must provide advice and assistance to help them find accommodation for themselves and secure suitable accommodation for them for a period that will give them a reasonable chance of doing so.

21. If, despite this assistance, homelessness persists, any children in the household could be in need under the Children Act 1989, and the family should be referred (with consent) to the children's social services authority.

Local connection and referrals to another authority

22. Broadly speaking, for the purpose of the homelessness legislation, people may have a local connection with a district because of residence, employment or family associations in the district, or because of special circumstances. (There are exceptions; for example, residence in a district while serving a prison sentence there does not establish a local connection.) Where applicants meet the criteria for the relief duty or for the main housing duty, and the authority considers that the applicant does not have a local connection with the district but does have one somewhere else, the housing authority dealing with the application can ask the housing authority in that other district to take responsibility for the case. However, applicants cannot be referred to another housing authority if they, or any member of their household, would be at risk of violence in the district of the other authority.

23. The definition of a 'local connection' for young people leaving care was amended by the Homelessness Reduction Act 2017 so that a young homeless care leaver has a local connection to the area of the local authority that looked after them. Additional provision is made for care leavers who have been placed in accommodation, under section 22A of the Children Act 1989, in a different district to that of the children's services authority that owes them leaving care duties. If they have lived in the other district for at least two years, including some time before they turned 16, they will also have a local connection with that district until they are 21.

Reviews and appeals

24. Housing authorities must provide written notifications to applicants when they reach certain decisions about their case, and the reasons behind any decisions that are against the applicant's interests. Applicants can ask the housing authority to review most aspects of their decisions, and, if still dissatisfied, can appeal to the county court on a point of law.

25. Housing authorities have the power to accommodate applicants pending a review or appeal to the county court. When an applicant who is being provided with interim accommodation requests a review of the suitability of accommodation offered to end the relief duty, the authority has a duty to continue to accommodate them pending a review.

23 February 2018

⇨ The above information is reprinted with kind permission from Gov. uk. Please visit www.gov.uk for further information.

© Crown copyright 2018

Six-year-old sets up Christmas campaign to help keep homeless people warm this winter

"I want to help all the homeless people in England."

By Amy Packham

A six-year-old boy who felt sad seeing people living out on the "freezing cold streets" is fundraising to buy hats, scarves and gloves for homeless people this Christmas.

Frankie Hill, from East London, was inspired to set up the campaign after having a conversation with his mum, Jane Brooks, about how, although Christmas is a "very fun" time for him and his family, some people don't get anything special at this time of year.

"I want to help all the homeless people in England," he told HuffPost UK.

"It makes me feel sad that some people don't get to do the same as me. Some people live on the streets, all alone and in the freezing cold."

Frankie has set himself the target of raising £1,000 for his JustGiving campaign 'Keep Warm With Frankie'.

"I would like to help keep [the homeless] warm this winter and have created a fundraising page (with the help of my family) so that I can raise enough money to afford some hats, scarves and gloves," he explained.

Explaining how the idea came about, Brooks said: "I was talking to Frankie about those who may not have so much this Christmas and the gift of giving, not just receiving and he decided he wanted to help people who might be homeless.

"He has been watching the total go steadily up and is very excited about being able to buy and distribute the winter woollies to those in need.

"I'm very proud of him."

At the time of writing, Frankie had raised £485 – nearly half of his target.

Frankie added that his favourite thing about Christmas is "when Santa comes".

4 December 2017

⇨ The above information is reprinted with kind permission from The Huffington Post UK. Please visit www.huffingtonpost.co.uk for further information.

How Denmark has helped its homeless young people

Our municipality now works with volunteers, housing specialists and social workers to give young homeless people all the support they need.

By Britta Martinsen, Head of Social Services for adults with special needs, Esbjerg

Since 2009, the national Danish strategy for tackling homelessness has been the housing first approach. We know it works – but it has not always worked well for our young people.

Housing first, which has also been used in Finland, involves substantial support from social care teams. We know from the figures we've collected that it works: of the 1,500 or so people in Denmark supported through the housing first scheme, nine out of ten have been able to keep their own home. Although we have seen an increase in homelessness in Denmark, the rise has been considerably lower in municipalities that have used the housing first approach compared with those that have not.

But a couple of years ago, we also realised that these results did not apply to our young citizens. Homelessness among 18- to 24-year-olds remains much too high. We wanted to make an extra effort for these young people.

We realised that many young people do not see themselves as 'homeless'. To them, a homeless person is a ragged man on a bench with a beer in his hand. Many young people without homes find a bed from day to day, in a friend's home, or with an acquaintance.

We found more young homeless women than we expected and particularly sad was that some of these young women have lived with men and supplied them with 'special' services, simply to get a place for the night.

We also saw a history of difficulties in many of these young people's lives and childhoods. Many of them had left school early, or had taken breaks from school. Many also suffered from substance abuse, were addicted to drugs, had committed crimes, and felt a lack of motivation.

In the Esbjerg municipality, our outreach services identified these young homeless people and assessed their needs. But we wanted to do something different. We did not want to make a new institution for these young people. We wanted them to have their own home from the start of our work with them, and we wanted to work with housing organisations and volunteers in NGOs.

So we set up a new project, with technical and economic support from Denmark's national board of social services, which has invested more than £250,000 in the project since June 2015.

Based on the housing first principles used in the national approach to tackling homelessness, we have created a partnership between the Esbjerg municipality, local housing associations, a shelter for homeless people, and an NGO called Hjemløses Venner – friends of the homeless.

The partnership provides young homeless people with small, low-cost apartments right away, without having to go and stay in temporary shelter first. The apartments are in ordinary areas, among other residents. In return, they have to assure us in writing that they will cooperate with the municipality and work with us and our partners. Making an intervention at the right time in these young people's lives is critically important in preventing young people from becoming homeless or from experiencing homelessness for further periods.

The NGO helps furnish the young person's apartment and make it into a home. It also offers support in a range of areas that the municipality itself would not cover, and helps these young people to create new and constructive networks.

After six months, we assess how people are doing, and decide whether they will be able to manage with the support from the volunteers, or whether they should get further support from our own specialist team.

They are then able to sign a regular contract on their apartment.

In the past 18 months, we have worked in this unique way with 15 young people. Two of them had so many issues that they needed more help and have been referred to a specialist institution. But all the rest of the young people we've worked with now have regular contracts for their own apartments.

Nicolai is 23 years old. Seven months ago he was a 'sofa-surfer'. He used a lot of drugs and had no real friends, but a lot of drug-related-acquaintances and huge debts. Now Nicolai has his own apartment and help to control his drug abuse, manage his money and make new friends. He says he now feels safe, calm and has control over his own life.

10 July 2017

⇨ The above information is reprinted with kind permission from *The Guardian*. Please visit www.theguardian.com for further information.

Record number of homeless alerts in freezing cold conditions – how you can help people sleeping rough in the snow

By Helena Horton

Arecord number of homeless alerts have been sent to a major charity as temperatures plummeted and snow blanketed most of the country.

More than 3,600 alerts were sent to the app StreetLink, which connects the homeless to local services, between Monday and Tuesday morning – the highest total ever for a 24-hour period.

This app allows concerned pedestrians to alert local authorities about people sleeping rough in the cold weather.

Councils have responded to the cold weather by providing extra beds, in order to ensure no one has to sleep outside in the snow, as the Met Office issued a "danger to life" red alert to parts of Scotland and the south west.

Around 500 extra beds in shelters, hostels and churches have been made available in the capital through local authorities, charities, faith and community groups after a *Swep* (Severe Weather Emergency Protocol) plan was triggered.

In response to the bitter conditions, St Mungo's homeless charity and the City of London have opened a new emergency shelter – in the Guild Church of Saint Mary Aldermary – which took in seven people on its first night.

St Mungo's has said London is experiencing its most prolonged period of freezing conditions for seven years, which could prove deadly for people sleeping outside.

One homeless man, Sam, was found by the charity just before midnight on a Wednesday in a London underpass, with no sleeping bag, set to sleep in just the clothes he was wearing.

He was taken to a shelter, and told the Press Association he was "very, very grateful", adding that he had felt "cold but relieved that someone was there, that someone actually cared", when

the St Mungo's workers approached him.

Asked how he had managed the cold, he said: "I've been walking around, but I find that I've got blisters on the bottom of my feet. I've been limping the past few days, it's not been good at all.

"I just want to get back on track."

Petra Salva, director of rough sleeper services, told PA that deaths on the streets over the bitterly cold snap were "a horrific possibility".

She said: "If we don't act, then people could die and ... we don't know yet what the consequences of this prolonged cold weather has been."

She said her mouth had "dropped open" after she walked into the church and saw a homeless person her team have been working with for four years, who, until now, had not accepted offers of a bed inside.

She said: "If tonight, he was the only one who came in, it would make it worthwhile."

But, she added, she was not comfortable with the idea that the doors would simply close on people as the emergency provisions end with the return of warmer weather.

She said: "The whole point of this is, yes, let's get people in and out of the dangerous weather conditions, but actually once we've got that opportunity, let's try and keep them in."

How you can help if you see a rough sleeper in this cold weather

Councils across the country have implemented Severe Weather Emergency Protocols for rough sleepers, meaning if passers-by report concerns to their local authority, they will send someone from the Rough Sleeper Team down to help.

Streetlink has asked concerned pedestrians to report the time, place and appearance of anyone sleeping rough in these temperatures.

A volunteer will then seek out the rough sleeper and offer them a warm bed for the night.

1 March 2018

Government to lead national effort to end rough sleeping

Sajid Javid sets out details of a new Rough Sleeping Advisory Panel that will help develop a national strategy.

By the Rt. Hon. Sajid Javid MP, and Alok Sharma MP

Communities Secretary Sajid Javid has today (30 November 2017) set out details of a new Rough Sleeping Advisory Panel that will help develop a national strategy as part of the Government's commitment to halve rough sleeping by 2022 and eliminate it altogether by 2027.

This new Advisory Panel made up of homelessness experts, charities and local government, will support the Ministerial Taskforce, which brings together ministers from key departments to provide a cross-government approach to preventing rough sleeping and homelessness.

Members of the Rough Sleeping Advisory Panel include:

⇨ Jon Sparkes, chief executive of Crisis, a leading charity focused on rough sleeping and single homelessness

⇨ Polly Neate, chief executive of homelessness charity Shelter, who brings her expertise on domestic abuse as a driver of homelessness

⇨ Jean Templeton, chief executive St Basil's, a West Midlands based charity that helps 16- to 25-year-olds who are homeless or at risk of homelessness

⇨ Mark Lloyd from the Local Government Association

⇨ Mayors for Manchester Andy Burnham and for the West Midlands Andy Street

⇨ Peter Fredriksson, a homelessness advisor to the Finnish Government, which has successfully piloted the Housing First approach.

This latest action builds on the work government is already doing including:

⇨ spending over £1 billion until 2020 to tackle homelessness and rough sleeping

⇨ implementing the Homelessness Reduction Act which will make sure more people get the help they need to prevent them from becoming homeless in the first place

⇨ £28 million of funding to pilot the Housing First approach for entrenched rough sleepers in the West Midlands Combined Authority, Greater Manchester, and the Liverpool City Region

⇨ investing £9 billion by March 2021 to build new affordable homes

⇨ a £20-million scheme to support homeless people and those at risk of homelessness secure homes in the private rented sector.

The Homelessness and Rough Sleeping Implementation Taskforce will be chaired by the Communities Secretary Sajid Javid.

Communities Secretary Sajid Javid said:

"No one should ever have to sleep rough. That's why this Government is committed to halving rough sleeping by 2022 and eliminating it altogether by 2027.

"To break the homelessness cycle once and for all, we all need to work together, drawing on as much expertise and experience as we can. The Homelessness and Rough Sleeping Implementation Taskforce and the Rough Sleeping Advisory Panel, together with the three Housing First pilots, are important steps in making that happen."

The Advisory Panel supporting the Taskforce will be chaired by the Homelessness Minister Marcus Jones.

Homelessness Minister Marcus Jones said:

"The Rough Sleeping Advisory Panel brings together experts with both the knowledge and determination to reduce homelessness and end rough sleeping.

"Working together with the charities and local authorities who have already achieved so much, we can fulfil our joint ambition to make sure we help some of the most vulnerable in society."

The Government is committed to reducing homelessness and rough sleeping, and making sure that individuals and families are provided with the support they need as early as possible. It is already spending over £1 billion until 2020 to tackle homelessness and rough sleeping.

Housing First

Communities Secretary Sajid Javid will take forward the implementation of the three Housing First pilots for which the budget confirmed the £28 million funding. The minister first saw the Housing First scheme on a fact-finding trip to Finland.

The pilots in Greater Manchester, the Liverpool City Region and the West Midlands Combined Authority will support the most entrenched rough sleepers get off the streets and help them to end their homelessness. Individuals will be provided with stable, affordable accommodation and intensive wrap-around support. This will help them to recover from complex health issues; for example

substance abuse and mental health difficulties, and sustain their tenancies.

Also announced in the budget is a new £20-million fund to support homeless people and those at risk of homelessness secure homes in the private rented sector.

Access to the private rented sector plays a part in both preventing and supporting the recovery from homelessness, helping people rebuild their lives. This fund could support bids for social lettings agencies, guaranteed deposit schemes or tenancy sustainment schemes. The department is keen to encourage bespoke, innovative solutions that reflect local need.

Government action to date on tackling homelessness and rough sleeping

⇨ Spending over £1 billion until 2020 to tackle homelessness and rough sleeping, part of which is our £50-million Homelessness Prevention Programme to deliver an 'end-to-end' approach to homelessness and rough sleeping prevention.

⇨ Implementing the Homelessness Reduction Act. The Act will significantly reform England's homelessness legislation, ensuring that more people get the help they need to prevent them from becoming homeless in the first place. The Act also ensures that other local services refer those either homeless or at risk of being homeless to local authority housing teams.

⇨ Investing £9 billion by March 2021 to build new affordable homes. This Government is committed to fixing the broken housing market and our Housing White Paper sets out measures to do just that.

⇨ £28-million funding to pilot the Housing First approach for entrenched rough sleepers in the West Midlands Combined Authority, Greater Manchester, and the Liverpool City Region.

New research into the causes of homelessness and rough sleeping

The Department for Communities and Local Government will be commissioning a feasibility study

which will explore whether it is possible to carry out robust and useful research on a complex issue such as the causes of homelessness.

Ministers have already confirmed plans to overhaul homelessness data to make sure we have a better picture of the homelessness challenge. As part of the implementation of the Homelessness Reduction Act, which requires councils to provide support much earlier to people at risk of becoming homeless, local authorities will collect a wider range of individual level data. This change from April 2018 will generate much richer data, helping both local and central government take the right action needed.

30 November 2017

⇨ The above information is reprinted with kind permission from Gov. uk. Please visit www.gov.uk for further information.

© Crown copyright 2018

Key facts

- The NAB counted 34,596 available places in hostel accommodation in 1966. The charity Homeless Link recorded 36,540 in 2014. (page 2)

- The number of households that have become homeless after an eviction over the past year is up 12% compared with a year ago at 18,820 while the total number of households in temporary accommodation has risen to 74,630, up 9% on a year earlier. Eviction by private landlord is now the most common cause of homelessness. (page 3)

- Homelessness in England has risen for the sixth year running, while temporary accommodation and B&B placements are up 52% and 250% respectively since 2009/10. (page 4)

- The autumn 2017 total number of rough sleepers counted and estimated was 4,751. (page 5)

- The number of rough sleepers increased by 173, or 18% in London and 444 or 14% in the rest of England since autumn 2016. (page 5)

- London represented 24% of the England total rough sleepers in autumn 2017. This is up from 23% of the England total in autumn 2016. (page 5)

- 14% of rough sleepers were women, 20% were non-UK nationals and 8% were under 25 years old. (page 5)

- Local authorities' counts and estimates show that 4,751 people slept rough in England on a snapshot night in autumn 2017. This is up 617 (15%) from the autumn 2016 total of 4,134. (page 5)

- Local councils have had to foot the bill for the soaring levels of homelessness, with most of the £1.1 billion spent on housing people in 2015/16 going on temporary accommodation, up by 39 per cent in real terms since 2010/11 – from £606 million to £845 million. (page 8)

- In the past 12 years, the rented sector as a whole has grown by a third, and the number of tenants being evicted from their homes has grown by a fifth: 7,200 more tenants lost their homes in 2015 than in 2003. (page 10)

- Over 40,000 tenants were evicted from their homes by landlords in 2015, and many more felt forced to move from their homes due to problems of affordability, the condition of the property, or disputes with their landlord. (page 10)

- New figures released by the charity Crisis show that the number of 'hidden' homeless will rise by 47% to 13,400 over the next decade, unless the Government takes immediate action. (page 12)

- The country needs to build 250,000 homes a year to keep up with demand. The last time housebuilding reached this level, in the 1970s, local government built around 40 per cent of them. (page 13)

- In most areas the rise in rents and house prices above earnings makes housing less affordable for a large and growing proportion of the population. (page 13)

- Rising rents make it increasingly difficult to buy a first home. Analysis from the LGA has revealed that one in seven private renters (14%) now spend more than half of their total income on rent. (page 14)

- Councils are currently housing 75,740 families including 118,960 children in temporary accommodation, at a net cost that has tripled in the last three years. (page 15)

- Since the onset of austerity in 2010, the estimated number of people sleeping rough in England has more than doubled, from 1,768 in 2010, to 4,134 in 2016. (page 27)

- In the period from 2006 to 2014, the number of court cases for 'vagrancy-related offences' in England increased by 70% – from 1,510 prosecutions to 2,365. (page 27)

- In 2017, there was a 15% rise in the number of people sleeping rough in the UK – and Westminster was no exception. In autumn 2017, Westminster was the local authority with the highest number of rough sleepers in England – 217 people. (page 29)

- A study for the homelessness charity Crisis found that 1,731 homeless people died in England between 2001 and 2009. (page 29)

- There are over 1,200 supporters and 23 homeless members on the platform who are pursuing a range of career paths – from electricians and accountants to teaching assistants and social workers. (page 30)

- Statistics from charity Shelter suggest there are more than 307,000 homeless people in Britain. (page 30)

- Under the Homelessness Act 2002, all housing authorities must have in place a homelessness strategy based on a review of all forms of homelessness in their district. The strategy must be renewed at least every five years. The social services authority must provide reasonable assistance. (page 32)

Begging

A beggar is someone who makes money by asking for donations from passers-by. Although begging and homelessness can be linked, not all rough sleepers beg or vice versa.

Bin death

Sometimes homeless people turn to sleeping in bins as a way to seek shelter and warmth. Unfortunately, these bins can be picked up by waste lorries, where the contents are loaded onto the on-board crushing equipment which can crush someone to death.

Hidden homelessness

In addition to those people recognised as statutory homeless, there are also a large number of homeless single adults, or couples without dependent children, who meet the legal definition of homelessness but not the criteria for priority need. In many cases they will not even apply for official recognition, knowing they do not meet the criteria. Statistics provided by the Government will therefore not include all people in the country who actually meet the definition of homelessness. As a result, this group is often referred to as the hidden homeless.

Homeless households

A family or individual who has applied for local authority housing support and been judged to be homeless.

Homelessness

The law defines somebody as being homeless if they do not have a legal right to occupy any accommodation or if their accommodation is unsuitable to live in. This can cover a wide range of circumstances, including, but not restricted to, the following: having no accommodation at all; having accommodation that is not reasonable to live in, even in the short-term (e.g. because of violence or health reasons); having a legal right to accommodation that for some reason you cannot access (e.g. if you have been illegally evicted); living in accommodation you have no legal right to occupy (e.g. living in a squat or temporarily staying with friends).

Homelessness and mental health

Mental health and housing are closely interlinked: mental ill health can make it difficult for people to maintain good quality housing and can lead to homelessness, whereas homelessness, poor quality housing and housing insecurity can lead to mental health issues. Mental ill health is common among people who experience homelessness and rough sleepers – estimates range from one-third up to 76%. An estimated 43% of clients in an average homelessness project in England are likely to have mental health needs.

Hostels and nightshelters

Hostels and nightshelters provide housing for people sleeping on the streets.

No Second Night Out

Launched on 1 April 2011, this is a project in London that aims to ensure that someone sleeping rough for the first time need not spend a second night out on the streets. NSNO helps people to return to their home area and be reconnected with their family and support networks. It is estimated that each week about 60 people are seen sleeping rough for the first time in London.

Priority need

Under homelessness legislation, certain categories of household are considered to have priority need for accommodation. Priority need applies to all households that contain a pregnant woman or are responsible for dependent children; to some households made up of a 16- to 17-year-old or a care leaver aged 18 to 21; or where someone is vulnerable, e.g. because of old age, health problems; or by having been in prison, care or the Forces.

Rough sleeping

A rough sleeper is a homeless person who is literally 'roofless' and lives predominantly on the streets.

Single homeless

This term refers to homeless individuals or couples without dependants.

Sofa surfing

When a person finds themselves without accommodation they rely on family and friends to put them up temporarily, usually sleeping on their sofa or floor, whilst they try to find more permanent accommodation.

Squatting

If a person is said to be squatting, it means they are occupying a property without the right to do so (e.g. they don't pay rent or own the property). Trespassing and squatting in residential buildings (like a house or flat) is illegal and is considered a crime (can lead to six months in prison, a £5,000 fine or both).

Assignments

Brainstorming

⇨ In small groups discuss what you know about homelessness?

- What does the term 'sofa-surfing' mean?
- What is a night shelter?
- What is rough-sleeping?
- What does the term eviction mean?
- What is hidden homelessness?

Research

⇨ Do some research into homelessness in the UK and the possible causes of it. You should consider which age groups and genders it affects and why. Write a short report and share with the rest of your class.

⇨ Conduct a questionnaire amongst your friends and family to find out how they feel about homeless people. Do they sympathise with them? Would they help them if they could and, if so, what sort of things would they do on a practical level. Write a report on your findings and share with your class.

⇨ Choose a country other than your own and, using the Internet, do some research to find out about homelessness in that country. Write some notes on your findings and feedback to your class.

⇨ In pairs, do some research into the number of children in the UK whom are living in temporary accommodation. What factors do you think have caused this? What is being done to help them and what more could be done? Write a report on your findings. This should cover at least one side of an A4 sheet.

⇨ Do some research into the types of accommodation young people experience, when they were without stable accommodation. Write a short report and share with your class.

Design

⇨ Imagine you work for a homeless charity. Design a poster to be displayed in public places such as bus stops and tube stations to highlight the plight of the homeless.

⇨ In pairs, design a night shelter.

⇨ Design a leaflet informing people about homelessness and its causes.

⇨ Choose an article from this book and design an illustration to highlight the key themes/message of your chosen article.

Oral

⇨ Read the article on page 19, 'Buy a homeless' project participants explain why they're happy to be 'sold'. As a class discuss the issues raised in this article. Do you think this is ethical? Is this a good way to draw attention to the plight of the homeless? What do you think could be done differently?

⇨ As a class, discuss the issue of homelessness. You should consider the reasons why people become homeless.

⇨ The article on page 7 says the number of homeless children in temporary accommodation soars 37%. In groups discuss what you think the causes are. What are your feelings about this? Share with the rest of your class.

⇨ Create a PowerPoint presentation that explores the different types of accommodation/options available to homeless people. Use some case studies to show the choices people sometimes make.

⇨ As a class, discuss the issue of eviction, Look at the reasons why people are evicted.

Reading/writing

⇨ Write a one-page definition of homelessness. Compare it to a classmates.

⇨ Write a one-page definition of eviction. Compare it to a classmates.

⇨ Choose one of the illustrations from this book and write a short report exploring the themes the artist has chosen to depict.

⇨ Find out what you can about rough sleepers in the UK and write a blog post exploring your feelings around the issue.

⇨ Read the article on page 23 about free sanitary products for the homeless. Write a letter to your local MP asking if free products could be made available in your locality. Explain why you feel this issue is important.

⇨ Imagine you are a mother who is in b and b accommodation. You have three young children and are finding the situation extremely difficult. Write a letter to your local council asking for help. You should explain what it is like to live in temporary accommodation, all together in one room, and why you feel you are entitled to help.

Acknowledgements

The publisher is grateful for permission to reproduce the material in this book. While every care has been taken to trace and acknowledge copyright, the publisher tenders its apology for any accidental infringement or where copyright has proved untraceable. The publisher would be pleased to come to a suitable arrangement in any such case with the rightful owner.

Images

All images courtesy of iStock except pages 7, Samantha-sophia and 37, Brandon-mathias; Unsplash

Illustrations

Don Hatcher: pages 12 & 28. Simon Kneebone: pages 2 & 39. Angelo Madrid: pages 19 & 36.

Additional acknowledgements

With thanks to the Independence team: Shelley Baldry, Danielle Lobban, Jackie Staines and Jan Sunderland.

Tina Brand

Cambridge, June 2018